TO
All from whom we have learned
and
all who will yet teach us

CRISIS INTERVENTION

Theory and methodology

CRISIS INTERVENTION

Theory and methodology

DONNA C. AGUILERA, R.N., M.S.

Associate Professor, Department of Nursing,
California State University at Los Angeles

JANICE M. MESSICK, R.N., M.S.

Program Evaluation Service,
Brentwood Veterans Administration Hospital,
Los Angeles

SECOND EDITION

The C. V. Mosby Company

SAINT LOUIS   1974

SECOND EDITION

Copyright © 1974 by The C. V. Mosby Company

All rights reserved. No part of this book may be reproduced
in any manner without written permission of the publisher.

Previous edition copyrighted 1970

Printed in the United States of America

Distributed in Great Britain by Henry Kimpton, London

Library of Congress Cataloging in Publication Data

Aguilera, Donna C
  Crisis intervention: theory and methodology.

  Includes bibliographies.
  1. Crisis intervention (Psychiatry). I. Messick,
Janice M., joint author. II. Title. [DNLM: 1. Cri-
sis intervention. WM420 A283c 1974]
RC480.5.A36 1974   616.8'91   73-22270
ISBN 0-8016-0093-6

VH/M/M 9 8 7 6 5 4 3 2 1

Foreword

It will soon be two decades since I wrote *Mental Health Manpower Trends* for the Joint Commission on Mental Illness and Health. It was a book which surveyed the nation's professional resources in the mental health field and found them sadly wanting. As part of the Commission I chaired the Task Force on Manpower. Since then I have come to reject the terms "mental illness" and "manpower" as being prejudicial and inappropriate. Terms such as mental disturbance, or mental disorder, or emotional disturbance seem to me to be ideologically more neutral, less supportive of the illness model. *Human resources* certainly is to be preferred to the more sexist term *manpower*. And *intervention* is better than *treatment*.

Anyway, in that survey I concluded that our nation did not have, and for the foreseeable future would not have, enough professionals in the conventional mental health fields to reach all the people who want, or are judged to require, intervention. Experience since then bears out the accuracy of this prediction. For example, despite a fourfold increase in the total membership of the American Psychiatric Association during the past 25 years, fewer psychiatrists are available now than then to the poor in the tax-supported institutions.

The mental health professions largely have concentrated their attention on the delivery of individual psychotherapy to persons who are predominantly affluent, white, Protestant, and female. In William Ryan's dramatic survey of mental health service delivery in Boston *(Distress in the City)* he found the typical psychiatric patient to be a white, middle-class, college-educated female between the ages of 30 and 40. Most of these "patients" were concentrated in a very small number of census tracts. Ryan found, too, that general practitioners, clergymen, and social agencies such as community centers were providing more intervention to the disturbed children and adults of Boston than were the traditional mental professions, despite the fact that Boston is Psychiatryland.

There are further problems with conventional mental health services. For one, many traditional clinics have a waiting list which delays the start of intervention for periods up to six months or a year. People in crisis situations want help now, not six months from now. This is particularly true of poor people with problems. They cannot send their kids to camp or take a trip to Europe while they wait for help.

Another sacred cow that needs to be hamburgerized is the belief of conventional agencies that meaningful intervention can be accomplished only by highly trained professional people possessing hard-to-get credentials that are based on extensive theoretical knowledge and often indoctrination into some particular school of therapy. Carl Rogers has recently blasted the whole credentials system for therapists. I agree with him, and believe that the research evidence supports the fact that some persons with little formal training are often as effective, or even more effective, in human intervention with disturbed people than are the experts.

Crisis intervention by a variety of people makes so much sense in so many ways. It sweeps aside the artificially created psychiatric and related personnel shortages by providing good, meaningful, and time-limited training to persons outside the traditional mental health professions. It provides support and help to people when it is needed, not months later to those lucky enough to survive a waiting list. It provides prompt access to help and so eliminates the dropping out that occurs in conventional systems between the move to seek help and the time it is available.

The authors have shown great skill and sensitivity in the preparation of this volume. Their blend of theory, history, and practical methods of crisis resolution should make the volume useful in a variety of training programs. It will be useful to both professionals and nonprofessionals. Its message should be heard and understood by legislators as well.

George W. Albee, Ph.D.
University of Vermont

Preface

We developed this textbook because we recognized the need for a comprehensive overview as well as an introduction and guide to crisis intervention from its historical development to its present utilization. Although the techniques and skills of a therapist must be learned and practiced under professional supervision, we believe that an awareness of the basic theory and principles of crisis intervention will be of value to all who are involved in the helping professions. It should be of particular value as a guideline to those in the mental health field who are in constant proximity to persons in stressful situations who seek help because they are unable to cope with them alone.

Since it was not our intent in the first edition of this textbook to imply that crisis intervention was limited only to the nursing profession, we have revised and added selected sections in response to our readers' requests.

Chapter 1 deals with the historical development of crisis intervention methodology. Its intent is to create awareness of the broad base of knowledge incorporated into present practice, the fundamental procedures of brief psychotherapy, and its implementation in community psychiatry.

Chapter 2 explores the differences between the psychotherapeutic techniques of psychoanalysis and psychoanalytic psychotherapy and between brief psychotherapy and crisis intervention methodology in the major areas of their goals, foci, activities of the therapists, indications for treatment, and the average lengths of treatment.

Chapter 3 presents an overview of therapeutic groups and group therapy to show the bases from which crisis groups evolve. Two recent studies on crisis groups are presented to show their implementation, advantages, and disadvantages, and a case study is included to demonstrate the use of crisis intervention techniques in a group therapy session.

Chapter 4 presents some of the sociocultural factors that can act as barriers in the psychotherapeutic process. The purpose of this chapter is to discuss certain key areas that are usually considered to be problems and to make the reader aware of the nature of these difficulties.

Chapter 5 focuses on the problem-solving process and introduces the reader to basic terminology used in this method of treatment. We have devised a paradigm of intervention for the purpose of clarifying the sequential steps of crisis development and crisis resolution and have included a brief case study to illustrate its application as a guide to case studies in subsequent chapters.

Chapter 6 deals with stressful events that could precipitate a crisis in individuals regardless of socioeconomic or sociocultural status. Hypothetical case studies based on factual experience are presented to illustrate the techniques used by therapists in crisis resolution. Theoretical material preceding each case study is presented as an overview relevant to the crisis situation.

Chapter 7 is devoted to those changes that occur during concomitant biological and social role transitions such as birth, puberty, young adulthood, marriage, illness or death of a family member, the climacteric, and old age. Maturational crisis have been described as normal processes of growth and development and differ from situational crisis in that they usually evolve over an extended period of time and frequently require more characterological changes of the individual. Case studies are included with appropriate theoretical material.

Chapter 8 provides an overview of the current trends in utilization of manpower resources in community mental health centers and of the research being conducted in crisis intervention.

We are indebted to many people who have been of direct and indirect assistance in writing this book. Specifically we wish to thank several persons for their roles in bringing the manuscript to fruition. We want to acknowledge our gratitude to Dr. G. F. Jacobson, Dr. W. E. Morley, and the Research Committee of the Los Angeles Psychiatric Service–Benjamin Rush Centers for their encouragement and advice. Our sincere thanks go to Dr. Evelyn Crumpton, Brentwood Veterans Administration Hospital, who served as our liaison with the Brentwood Research Committee, to Mrs. Betty Connolly, Medical Librarian, Sepulveda Veterans Administration Hospital, who assisted in our research of the literature, and to Steven Farrow for the cover idea. We are especially grateful to Mrs. Jean Hansen, without whose valuable and expert assistance the manuscript could not have been prepared in its final form. To our families, who were our kindest critics and strongest supporters, we owe a very special kind of debt.

D. C. A.
J. M. M.

Contents

1   Historical development of crisis intervention methodology

A person in crisis is at a turning point. He faces a problem that he cannot readily solve by using the coping mechanisms that have worked for him before. As a result, his tension and anxiety increase, and he becomes less able to find a solution. A person in this situation feels helpless—he is caught in a state of great emotional upset and feels unable to take action *on his own* to solve his problem.

Crisis intervention can offer the immediate help that a person in crisis needs in order to reestablish equilibrium. This is an inexpensive, short-term therapy that focuses on solving the immediate problem. Increasing awareness of sociocultural factors that could precipitate crisis situations has led to the rapid evolution of crisis intervention methodology. Therefore, these factors will be discussed first in order to understand their social and cultural implications better.

Everywhere today we hear talk of the changes in our lives that have been made by "urbanization" and "technology." A closer study of these changes will add to our understanding of what they have meant to families and to individuals.

Before the revolution in technology and industrialization, most people lived on farms or in small rural communities. They were chiefly self-employed, either on their farms or in small, associated businesses. When sons and daughters married, they were likely to remain near their parents, working in the same occupations, and in this way, trades and occupations were a link between generations. Families therefore tended to be large, and because family members lived and worked together and relied chiefly upon each other for social interaction they developed strong loyalties and a sense of responsibility for one another.

Contemporary urban life, however, does not encourage or allow this kind of sheltered, close-knit family relationship. People who live in cities are likely to be employed by a company and paid a wage. They work with business associates and live with neighbors rather than with their immediate family. Because of housing conditions and the necessity of living on a wage, families in cities usually consist of parents and unmarried children.

These differences between rural and urban life have important repercussions with regard to individual security and stability. The large, extended rural family offered a large and relatively constant group of associates. Family size and the varying strength of blood ties meant that there was always someone to talk to, even about a problem involving two family members. But urban life is highly mobile. There is often a rapid turnover in business associates and neighbors, and there is no certainty that these relative strangers will share the same values, beliefs, and interests. All these factors make it difficult for people to develop real trust and interdependence outside the small immediate family. In addition, urban life requires that people meet each other only superficially, in specific roles and in limited relationships rather than as total personalities.

All of these factors taken together mean that people in cities are more isolated than ever before from the emotional support provided by the family and close and familiar peers. As a result, there are no role models to follow—the demands of urban life are constantly changing, and coping behavior that was appropriate and successful several years before may be hopelessly ineffective today.

This creates a favorable environment for the development of crises. As defined by Caplan,[1] crisis may occur when the individual faces a problem that he cannot solve. There is a rise in inner tension and signs of anxiety and inability to function in extended periods of emotional upset.

HISTORICAL DEVELOPMENT

The crisis approach to therapeutic intervention has been developed only within the past few decades and is based upon a broad range of theories of human behavior, including those of Freud, Hartmann, Rado, Erickson, Lindemann, and Caplan. Its current acceptance as a recognized form of treatment cannot be directly related to any single theory of behavior; all have contributed to some degree.

Our intent in presenting an overview of historical development is to create awareness of the broad base of knowledge incorporated into present practice. Although not all theories of human behavior are necessarily dependent on Freudian concepts, and only a selected few are presented here, we chose to begin with the psychoanalytic theories of Freud because these are a major basis for further investigation of normal and abnormal human behavior. The fundamental procedures of brief psychotherapy are derived from hypotheses based upon studies of the reasons for normal as well as abnormal human behavior.

Sigmund Freud was the first to demonstrate and apply the principle of causality as it relates to psychic determinism.[2] Simply put, this principle states that every act

---

[1]Caplan, Gerald: An approach to community mental health, New York, 1961, Grune & Stratton, Inc., p. 18.
[2]Bellak, Leopold, and Small, Leonard: Emergency psychotherapy and brief psychotherapy, New York, 1965, Grune & Stratton, Inc., p. 6.

of human behavior has its cause, or source, in the history and experience of the individual. It follows that causality is operative, whether or not the individual is aware of the reason for his behavior. Psychic determinism is the theoretical foundation of psychotherapy and psychoanalysis. The technique of free association, dream interpretation, and the assignment of meaning to symbols are all based upon the assumption that causal connections operate unconsciously.

A particularly important outcome of Freud's deterministic position was his construction of a developmental or "genetic" psychology.[3] Present behavior is understandable in terms of the life history or experience of the individual, and the crucial foundations for all future behavior are laid down in infancy and early childhood. The most significant determinants of present behavior are the "residues" of past experiences (learned responses), particularly those developed during the earliest years to reduce biological tensions.

Freud assumed that a reservoir of energy that exists in the individual initiates all behavior. Events function as guiding influences, but they do not initiate behavior; they only serve to help mold it in certain directions.[4]

Since the end of the nineteenth century, the concept of determinism, as well as the scientific bases from which Freud formulated his ideas, have undergone many changes.

Although the ego-analytic theorists have tended to subscribe to much in the Freudian position, there are several respects in which they differ. These seem to be extensions of Freudian theory rather than direct contradictions. As a group, they conclude that Freud has neglected the direct study of normal or healthy behavior.[5]

Heinz Hartmann was an early ego analyst who was profoundly versed in Freud's theoretical contributions.[6] He postulated that the psychoanalytic theories of Freud could prove valid for normal as well as pathological behavior. Hartmann began with the study of ego functions and distinguished between two groups: those that develop from conflict, and the others, "conflict free," such as memory, thinking, and language, which he labeled "primary autonomous functions of the ego." He considered these important in the adaptation of the individual to his environment. Hartmann emphasized that man's adaptation in early childhood as well as his ability to maintain his adaptation to his environment in later life had to be considered. His conception of the ego as an organ of adaptation required further study of the concept of reality. He also described man searching for an environment as another form of adaptation—the fitting together of the individual and his society. He believed that although the behavior of the individual is strongly influenced by his culture, a part of the personality remains relatively free of this influence.

[3]Ford, Donald, and Urban, Hugh: Systems of psychotherapy, New York, 1963, John Wiley & Sons, Inc., p. 117.

[4]Ibid., p. 178.

[5]Ibid., p. 181.

[6]Loewenstein, Rudolph M.: Psychology of the ego. In Alexander, F., Eisenstein, S., and Grotjahn, M., editors: Psychoanalytic pioneers, New York, 1966, Basic Books, Inc., Publishers, p. 475.

Sandor Rado developed the concept of adaptational psychodynamics, providing a new approach to the unconscious as well as new goals and techniques of therapy.[7] Rado saw human behavior as being based upon the dynamic principle of motivation and adaptation. An organism achieves adaptation through interaction with its culture. Behavior is viewed in terms of its effect upon the welfare of the individual, not just in terms of cause and effect. The organism's patterns of interaction improve through adaptation, with the goal being the increase of possibilities for survival. Freud's classical psychoanalytic technique emphasized the developmental past and the uncovering of unconscious memories, and little if any importance was attached to the reality of the present. Rado's[8] adaptational psychotherapy, however, emphasizes the immediate present without neglecting the influence of the developmental past. Primary concern is with failures in adaptation "today," what caused them, and what the patient must do to learn to overcome them. Interpretations always begin and end with the present; preoccupation with the past is discouraged. As quickly as insight is achieved, it is used as a beginning to encourage the patient to enter into his present, real-life situation repeatedly. Through practice the patient automatizes new patterns of healthy behavior. According to Rado, it is this automatization factor that is ultimately the curative process, not insight. He does not believe that it takes place passively in the doctor's office but actively in the reality of daily living.

Erik H. Erikson further developed the theories of ego psychology, which complement those of Freud, Hartmann, and Rado, by focusing on the epigenesis of the ego and on the theory of reality relationships.[9] Epigenetic development is characterized by an orderly sequence of development at particular stages, each depending upon the other for successful completion. Erikson perceived eight stages of psychosocial development, spanning the entire life cycle of man and involving specific developmental tasks that must be solved in each phase. The solution that is achieved in each previous phase is applied in subsequent phases. Erikson's theory is important in that it offers an explanation of the individual's social development as a result of his encounters with his social environment. Another significant feature is his elaboration on the normal rather than the pathological development of man's social interactions. He dealt in particular with the problems of adolescence and saw this period in life as a "normative crisis," that is, a normal maturational phase of increased conflicts, with apparent fluctuations in ego strength.[10] Erikson integrated

---

[7]Salzman, Leon: Developments in psychoanalysis, New York, 1962, Grune & Stratton, Inc., pp. 124-125.

[8]Ovesy, Lionel, and Jameson, Joan: Adaptational techniques of psychodynamic therapy. In Rado, S., and Daniels, G., editors: Changing concepts of psychoanalytic medicine, New York, 1956, Grune & Stratton, Inc., pp. 165-178.

[9]Rappaport, David: A historical survey of phychoanalytic ego psychology. In Klein, G. S., editor: Psychological issues, New York, 1959, International Universities Press, p. 14.

[10]Pumpian-Mindlin, Eugene: Contributions to the theory and practice of psychoanalysis and psychotherapy. In Alexander, Eisenstein, and Grotjahn, editors: Psychoanalytic pioneers, p. 475.

the biological, cultural, and self-deterministic points of view in his eight stages of man's development and broadened the scope of traditional psychotherapy with his theoretical formulations concerning identity and identity crises. His theories have provided a basis for the work of others who further developed the concept of maturational crises and began serious consideration of situational crises and man's adaptation to his current environmental dilemma.

Lindemann's[11] initial concern was in developing approaches that might contribute to the maintenance of good mental health and the prevention of emotional disorganization on a community-wide level. He chose to study bereavement reactions in his search for social events or situations that predictably would be followed by emotional disturbances in a considerable portion of the population. In his study of bereavement reactions among the survivors of those killed in the Coconut Grove nightclub fire, he described both brief and abnormally prolonged reactions occurring in different individuals as a result of a loss of a significant person in their lives.[12]

In his experiences in working with grief reactions, Lindemann concluded that it might be profitable for investigation and useful for the development of preventive efforts if a conceptual frame of reference were to be constructed around the concept of an emotional crisis, as exemplified by bereavement reactions. Certain inevitable events in the course of the life cycle of every individual can be described as hazardous situations, for example, bereavement, the birth of a child, marriage, and so forth. He postulated that in each of these situations emotional strain would be generated, stress would be experienced, and a series of adaptive mechanisms would occur that could lead either to mastery of the new situation or to failure with more or less lasting impairment to function. Although such situations create stress for all people who are exposed to them, they become crises for those individuals who by personality, previous experience, or other factors in the present situation are especially vulnerable to this stress and whose emotional resources are taxed beyond their usual adaptive resources.

Lindemann's theoretical frame of reference led to the development of crisis intervention techniques, and in 1946 he and Caplan established a community-wide program of mental health in the Harvard area, called the Wellesley Project.

According to Caplan,[13] the most important aspects of mental health are the state of the ego, the stage of its maturity, and the quality of its structure. Assessment of its state is based upon three main areas: (1) the capacity of the person to withstand stress and anxiety and to maintain ego equilibrium, (2) the degree of reality recognized and faced in solving problems, and (3) the repertoire of effective

---

[11]Lindemann, Erich: The meaning of crisis in individual and family, Teachers Coll. Rec. **57:** 310, 1956.
[12]Ibid., p. 311.
[13]Caplan: An approach to community mental health, pp. 34-37.

coping mechanisms employable by the person in maintaining a balance in his psychobiosocial field.

Caplan believes that all the elements that compose the total emotional milieu of the person must be assessed in an approach to preventive mental health. The material, physical, and social demands of reality, as well as the needs, instincts, and impulses of the individual, must all be considered as important behavioral determinants.

As a result of his work in Israel (1948)[14] and his later experiences in Massachusetts with Lindemann and with the Community Mental Health Program at Harvard University, he evolved the concept of the importance of *crisis* periods in individual and group development.

Crisis is defined as occurring "when a person faces an obstacle to important life goals that is, for a time, insurmountable through the utilization of customary methods of problem solving. A period of disorganization ensues, a period of upset, during which many abortive attempts at solution are made."[15]

In essence, the individual is viewed as living in a state of emotional equilibrium, with his goal always to return to or to maintain that state. When customary problem-solving techniques cannot be used to meet the daily problems of living, the balance or equilibrium is upset. The individual must either solve the problem or adapt to nonsolution. In either case a new state of equilibrium will develop, sometimes better and sometimes worse insofar as positive mental health is concerned. There is a rise in inner tension, there are signs of anxiety, and there is disorganization of function, resulting in a protracted period of emotional upset. This he refers to as "crisis." The outcome is governed by the kind of interaction that takes place during that period between the individual and the key figures in his emotional milieu.

EVOLUTION OF COMMUNITY PSYCHIATRY

Community psychiatry is, even now, emerging as a new field. New concepts and new psychobiosocial problems arise continually in rapidly changing cultures so that it is a broad, fluid field. A difference is now perceived between long-term, psychoanalytic therapy of the individual and short-term, reality-oriented psychotherapy as practiced in community psychiatry.

In the middle 1960's the term crisis intervention was not yet included in psychiatric dictionaries. In 1970 the fourth edition of Hinsie and Campbell's *Psychiatric Dictionary* listed crisis intervention as one of several modes of community psychiatry: "In the crisis-intervention model, the focus is on transitional-situational demands for novel adaptational responses. Because minimal intervention at such times tends to achieve maximal and optimal effects, such

---

[14]Caplan, Gerald: A public health approach to child psychiatry, Mental Health **35:**235-249, 1951.
[15]Caplan: An approach to community mental health, p. 18.

a model is more readily applicable to population groups than the medical model."[16]

According to Bellak (1964), community psychiatry evolved from multiple disciplines and is intrinsically bound to the development of psychoanalytic theory. The social and behavioral sciences that advanced during the first half of this century were predicated on psychodynamic hypotheses. At the same time, concepts of public health and epidemiology were advancing in community health programs.

After World War II the general public's increasing awareness and acceptance of the high incidence of psychiatric problems created changes in attitudes and demands for community action.

The discovery and utilization of psychotropic drugs was an important step forward. This resulted in opportunities for open wards and rehabilitation of the hospitalized patient in his home milieu.

It would be incorrect to assume that all of these factors merged spontaneously, creating a successful, structured cure for psychiatric illness. Rather, this was a slow process of trial and error. Widely different programs, each striving to meet problems involving different cultures, interests, knowledge, and skills, communicated and related to other programs similarly initiated. Disciplines once separated in goals became cognizant of their interdependence in attaining mutually recognized goals. New, allied disciplines developed; roles changed and expanded. There was a diffusion of tasks, and lines between disciplines became more flexible.

The origin of day hospitals for the care of psychiatric patients grew out of a shortage of hospital beds[17] (which forced premature discharges of patients to their homes) rather than as a treatment innovation. The first reported day hospital was associated with the First Psychiatric Hospital in Moscow in 1933. As Dzhagarov[18] states: "The need to continue treatment and for special observation in a setting similar to that of a hospital suggested a practical solution in the form of admission to the preventive section of the hospital. In a short time a transformation took place, the day hospital was created, proving to be adequately prepared to meet the new needs." In referring to this day hospital in Moscow, Kramer, as quoted by Ross,[19] says: "While this day center is little known and probably had little effect on later developments in the Western world, it is accurate to say that this was the first organized Day Hospital for individuals with severe mental illness."

In the late 1930's Bierer[20] began the Marlborough Experiment in England.

---

[16]Hinsie, L. E., and Campbell, R. J.: Psychiatric dictionary, ed. 4, New York, 1970, Oxford University Press, Inc., p. 606.

[17]Ross, Matthew: Extramural treatment techniques. In Bellak, L., editor: Handbook of community psychiatry and community mental health, New York, 1964, Grune & Stratton, Inc., p. 190.

[18]Dzhagarov, M. A.: Experience in organizing a day hospital for mental patients, Neuropathologia Psikhiatria **6:**147, 1937. (Translated for authors by G. Wachbrit.)

[19]Ross: Extramural treatment techniques, p. 190.

[20]Bierer, Joshua: The Marlborough experiment. editor: Handbook of community psychiatry and community mental health, pp. 221-247.

Patients, as members of a "therapeutic social club," lived outside the hospital and were treated at day hospitals or part-time facilities. According to Bierer, the primary goal of the program was to change the patient's concept of his role from that of a passive object of treatment to one of an active participant-collaborator. At the same time, the psychiatrist and his staff had to reconceptualize the patient as a human being accessible to reason, emphasizing his assets rather than concentrating on his psychopathology and conflicts. The reality of here and now was the focus of attention.

These innovations in attitude gave rise to the concept of "therapeutic community." The patient became a partner and collaborator with the staff and was granted equal rights, opportunities, and facilities. The medical staff and their assistants functioned as advisors.

The patient group assumed responsibility for the behavior of its members, as well as planning for activities, planning their futures, and offering support to each other. Group and social methods that encouraged the constant interaction of the members were used.

Other complementary projects developed in the Marlborough Program were the Day Hospital, the Night Hospital, the Aftercare Rehabilitation Center, the Self-Governed Community Hostel, Neurotics Nomine, and the Weekend Hospital.

Linn[21] describes Cameron's first day hospital in Montreal (1946), in which he and others were responsible for defining and giving formal structure to the program as a treatment innovation.

With this frame of reference it was only natural that the general hospital should add to the various roles in which it serves the community—that of becoming a focal point of preventive medicine and public health functions in psychiatry.

In 1958 a "Trouble Shooting Clinic" was initiated by Bellak[22] as part of City Hospital of Elmhurst, New York, a general hospital with 1,000 beds. The clinic was designed to offer first aid to emotional problems and was not limited to urgent crises. It combined two aspects of service: major emergencies as well as minor problems involving guidance, legal problems, and marital relations on a walk-in basis around the clock.

After the passage of the California Community Mental Health Act (1958) the California Department of Mental Hygiene established the first state agency in the country (1961) to undertake the training of specialists in community psychiatry.

It was recognized that clinics were needed to accommodate those individuals in the community who were unfamiliar with established forms of psychiatric treatment. A cause for these individuals' exclusion from treatment conceivably could

---

[21]Linn, Louis: Psychiatric program in a general hospital. In Bellak, editor: Handbook of community psychiatry and community mental health, 138.

[22]Bellak, Leopold: A general hospital as a focus of community psychiatry, J.A.M.A. **174:**2214, 1960.

have been due to divergency in social-cultural background, lack of communication, and lack of recognition of the need for services by both the population and the existing agencies.

In January, 1962, the Benjamin Rush Center for Problems of Living, a division of the Los Angeles Psychiatric Service, was opened as a no-waiting, unrestricted intake, walk-in crisis intervention center.

In 1967 crisis intervention replaced emergency detention at the San Francisco General Hospital. On each of the psychiatric units interdisciplinary teams were established whose primary goals were to reestablish independent functioning of the clients as soon as possible. In a follow-up study in 1972, Decker and Stubblebine[23] concluded that the crisis-intervention program achieved the anticipated reduction in psychiatric inpatient treatment.

In the early 1970's the Bronx Mental Health Center[24] (Centro de Hygiene Mental del Bronx) was created for crisis intervention for the low socioeconomic Spanish-speaking people and was staffed by Spanish-speaking psychiatrists.

At about the same time, brief crisis-intervention services were being offered by suburban churches in Montreal, Canada,[25] on an experimental basis. The goal of the program was to reach families undergoing a variety of stress through a roving walk-in clinic. The clinics served to facilitate delivery of these services to a latent population at risk, not reached by other means and at a point early in the evolution of a life crisis.

The first hot line was started at Children's Hospital in Los Angeles in 1968. Hot lines and youth crisis centers have been created in recognition of the failure of traditional approaches to make contacts among adolescents. Twenty-four–hour crisis telephones, free counseling with a minimum of red tape, walk-in contacts, crash pads, and young people serving as volunteer staff in such services are becoming increasingly attractive to the youth who are emerging as the locus of a counterculture.

Trends such as these are being repeated around the country as community mental health programs recognize the value of providing services in primary and secondary prevention unique to the needs of their particular clients. Increasing recognition is also being given to the need to provide more services for those clients whose needs are for continuing support in rehabilitation after resolution of the immediate crisis.

---

[23]Decker, J. B., and Stubblebine, J. M.: Crisis intervention and prevention of psychiatric disability; a follow-up study, Am. J. Psychiatry **129**:101-105, Dec. 1972.

[24]Morales, H. M.: Bronx Mental Health Center, N. Y. State Division Bronx Bull. **13**(8):6, 1971.

[25]Lecker, S., and others: Brief intervention; a pilot walk-in clinic in suburban churches, Can. Psychiatr. Assoc. J. **16**(2):141-146, 1971.

ADDITIONAL READINGS

Bellak, L., and Barten, H., editors: Progress in community mental health, New York, Grune & Stratton, Inc.; vol. 1, 1969; vol. 2, 1972.

Clark, Ted, and Jaffe, Dennis T.: Change within youth crisis centers, Am. J. Orthopsychiatry **42:**675-687, July 1972.

Community mental health services in Northern Europe, U. S. Department of Health, Education and Welfare, Public Health Service, Washington, D. C., 1965, U. S. Government Printing Office.

De Smit, N. W.: Crisis intervention and crisis centers; their possible relevance for community psychiatry and mental health care, Psychiat. Neurol. Neurochir. **75:**299-301, 1972.

De Smit, N. W.: The crisis center in community psychiatry; an Amsterdam experiment, Curr. Psychiatr. Ther., 1971, pp. 195-197.

Evans, F. M. C.: The role of the nurse in community mental health, New York, 1968, The Macmillan Co.

Freeman, Hugh, and Farndale, James: Trends in mental health services, New York, 1963, The Macmillan Co.

Glasscote, Raymond, and others: The community mental health center, an analysis of existing models, Washington, D. C., 1964, The Joint Information Service of the American Psychiatric Association and the National Association for Mental Health.

Gruenberg, Ernest M., editor: Evaluating the effectiveness of community mental health services, New York, 1966, Milbank Memorial Fund.

Hall, Calvin S., and Lindzey, Gardner: Theories of personality, ed. 2, New York, 1970, John Wiley & Sons, Inc.

Hankoff, L. D.: Emergency psychiatric treatment, Springfield, Ill., 1968, Charles C Thomas, Publisher.

Kier, Ari, editor: Psychiatry in the Communist world, New York, 1968, Science House, Inc.

Meltzoff, Julian, and Blumenthal, Richard L.: The day treatment center, Springfield, Ill., 1966, Charles C Thomas, Publisher.

Munroe, Ruth L.: Schools of psychoanalytic thought, New York, 1955, Holt, Rinehart & Winston, Inc.

Nemiah, John C.: Foundations of psychopathology, New York, 1961, Oxford University Press, Inc.

Rhine, Mark W., and Mayerson, Peter: Crisis hospitalization within a psychiatric emergency service, Am. J. Psychiatry **127**(10):1386-1391, 1971.

Roberts, Leigh M., and others, editors: Community psychiatry, Madison, Wis., 1966, University of Wisconsin Press.

Schneidman, Edwin S., and Farberow, Norman L.: The cry for help, New York, 1961, Blakiston Division, McGraw-Hill Book Co.

Straker, Manuel: Brief psychotherapy in an outpatient clinic; evaluation and evolution, Am. J. Psychiatry **124:**1219-1226, March 1968.

Straker, Manuel, and others: A comprehensive emergency psychiatric service in a general hospital, Can. Psychiatr. Assoc. J. **16:**137-139, April 1971.

Torop, Paul, and Torop, Karen: Hot lines and youth culture values, Am. J. Psychiatry **129:**730-733, Dec. 1972.

Wepman, Joseph M., and Heine, Ralph W., editors: Concepts of personality, Chicago, 1963, Aldine Publishing Co.

2 Differentiation between psychotherapeutic techniques

Psychotherapy as a form of treatment has had many definitions, some conflicting and others concurring. Areas of divergence are generally those of methodology, therapeutic goals, length of therapy, and indications for treatment. All apparently agree that psychotherapy is a set of procedures for changing behaviors based primarily on the establishment of a relationship between two (or more) people.

PSYCHOANALYSIS AND PSYCHOANALYTIC PSYCHOTHERAPY

The original theories of Sigmund Freud, the founder of psychoanalysis, passed through several phases as he subjected changing hypotheses to the tests of experience and observation, all directed toward the goal of making the unconscious available to the conscious.

In collaboration with Breuer, Freud first developed the psychotherapeutic technique of "cathartic hypnosis." Recognizing that ego control of the unconscious was released under the influence of hypnosis, Freud used hypnotism to induce the patient to answer direct questions in an effort to uncover the unconscious causes of his symptomatology and to allow free expression of pent-up feelings.

Freud observed, however, that to obtain therapetuic results the procedure had to be repeated. He recognized that material brought to consciousness during hypnosis returned to the unconscious as the awakening patient regained control over his emotions. The therapeutic task of making the conscious patient recall and face repressed emotions in order to gain insight and increased ego strength was only transiently achieved by this technique.

Freud then experimented with what he referred to as "waking suggestion." Laying his hand on the patient's forehead, he would strongly suggest that the patient could recall the past if he tried. He soon learned that a person could not be forced to recall repressed, conflictual emotional events through this approach.

He next devised an indirect method of freeing unconsciously repressed material for confrontation by the conscious. Using the process of "free association," the patient was expected to verbalize whatever thoughts came into his mind, freely associating events from his whole life span of experiences, feelings, fantasies, and dreams without concern for logic or continuity. Freud concentrated upon gaining an intellectual understanding of the patient's psychogenic past. He insisted upon the "basic rule" that the patient tell the therapist everything that came into his mind during each interview. Nothing, no matter how inconsequential the patient might think it was, could be withheld from the analyst. In this process of a search for re-pressed memories he found that repressed emotions were gradually discharged as they emerged, although not as dramatically as in cathartic hypnosis.

One of the most important discoveries by Freud is considered to be "transfer-ence phenomena." He deemed transference to be a valuable therapeutic tool in overcoming the patient's defenses in resisting the release of unconscious, repressed emotional experiences. He thought of transference as an emotional reaction of the patient to the therapist in which the patient would relive his conflicts and emotions as they emerged from the past, from his unconscious. He would transfer to the therapist emotions that he had felt toward authority figures in his childhood.

Freud referred to this reliving of the neurotic past in a present relationship with the therapist as transference neurosis. The principal factor in this process was that the patient expressed his aggressions against the therapist without any fears of the reprisal or censure that he may have been subjected to by the authority figure in his childhood. Through the therapist's nonjudgmental acceptance the patient was encouraged to face new material released from his own unconscious with reduced fear and anxiety. As these new experiences were assimilated into the conscious ego, coping skills increased. This in turn facilitated further release of repressed material. Alexander[1] refers to this process as a "corrective emotional experience."

Psychoanalysis is concerned with theory as well as techniques. Alexander and French[2] also state that the traditional approach in psychoanalytic therapy has been nondirective. The therapist is a passive observer who would follow the lead of the patient's verbal expressions as they unfolded before him. Tarachow (1963) indi-cates that psychoanalytic therapy is for those whose personalities and ego strengths are relatively intact, despite neurotic symptoms or mild to moderately severe characterological disturbances due to unconscious conflicts.

Stone[3] lists eight factors in the situation and technique of psychoanalysis from

---

[1]Alexander, Franz: Psychoanalysis and psychotherapy, New York, 1956, W. W. Norton & Co., Inc., p. 41.

[2]Alexander, Franz, and French, Thomas M.: Psychoanalytic therapy, New York, 1946, The Ronald Press Co., p. 5.

[3]Stone, Leo: Psychoanalysis and brief psychotherapy, Psychoanal. Q. **20:**217-218, 1951.

which technical variations have derived: "(1) Practically exclusive reliance during the hour on the patient's free associations for communication; (2) regularity of the time, frequency and duration of appointments and a clearly defined financial agreement; (3) three to five appointments a week (originally six), with daily appointments the dominant tendency; (4) recumbent position, in most instances with some impediment against seeing the analyst directly; (5) confinement of the analyst's activity essentially to interpretation or other purely informative interventions such as reality testing, or an occasional question; (6) the analyst's emotional passivity and neutrality (benevolent objectivity), specifically abstention from gratifying the analysand's transference wishes; (7) abstention from advice or any other direct intervention or participation in the patient's daily life; (8) no immediate emphasis on curing symptoms, the procedure being guided largely by the patient's free associations from day to day. In a sense the analyst regards the whole scope of the patient's psychic life as his field of observation."

In psychoanalytic psychotherapy the therapist is more active than in psychoanalysis. He interacts more with the patient and does not interpret the transference attitudes as completely as in analysis. His most helpful attitude is one of calmness, continued interest, and sympathetic, understanding helpfulness. This differs from the neutral attitude of the analyst in psychoanalysis. Contention is that this calm, helpful, interested attitude of the therapist in psychotherapy provides support for the patient in dealing with his tensions, sustains his contact with reality, and provides gratifications and rewards in the therapeutic relationship. These, in turn, provide incentives for the patient to continue to deal with emerging unconscious material.

Freud (1924) expressed the opinion that any digression from classical psychoanalysis which still recognizes the two basic facts of transference and resistance and takes them as the starting point of its work may call itself psychoanalysis, even though it arrives at results other than his own.

Alexander (1956) has noted that in procedures which deviate from the classical psychoanalysis of Freud, one or another of the basic phenomena is emphasized from the standpoint of therapeutic significance and is often being dealt with in isolation from others. For example, Rank centered on the life situation, believing that insight into infantile history had no therapeutic significance. Ferenczi placed emphasis on the emotional experience in transference (abreaction factor). Reich concentrated on the analysis of the resistances in order to allow, by their removal, the discharge of highly charged emotional experiences. He emphasized the importance of hidden forms of resistance and the understanding of the patient's behavior apart from his verbal communication.[4]

Psychoanalytic psychotherapy procedures have customarily been divided into two functional categories based upon methodology; these are frequently referred

---

[4]Alexander: Psychoanalysis and psychotherapy, pp. 53-55.

to as supportive (suppressive) and uncovering (exploratory or expressive) procedures.

According to Alexander,[5] the aim of the uncovering procedure is to intensify the ego's ability to handle repressed emotional conflict situations that are unconscious. Through the use of transference the patient relives his early interpersonal conflicts in relation to the therapist. Supportive and uncovering procedures overlap, but it is not difficult to differentiate between them. Primarily, supportive methods of treatment are indicated when functional impairment of the ego is temporary in nature and caused by acute emotional distress. Alexander designated therapeutic tasks in supportive methodology as follows: (1) gratifying dependency needs of the patient during stress situations, thereby reducing anxiety; (2) reducing stress by giving the patient an opportunity for abreaction; (3) giving intellectual guidance by objectively reviewing with the patient his acute stress situation and assisting him in making judgments, thereby enabling him to gain proper perspective of the total situation; (4) supporting the patient's neurotic defenses until the ego can handle the emotional discharges; and (5) actively participating in manipulation of the life situation when this might be the only hopeful approach in the given circumstances.

Psychoanalysis and psychoanalytic psychotherapy require many years of intensive training on the part of the therapist; this in itself has limited the number of therapists available. Both methods may require that the individual remain in therapy over an extended period of time, often for years. The obligation of time as well as expense for such extensive treatment also limits its availability for many.

BRIEF PSYCHOTHERAPY

Brief psychotherapy as a treatment form developed as the result of the increased demand for mental health services and the lack of personnel trained to meet this demand. Initially, much of it was conducted by psychiatric residents as part of their training. Later, psychiatric social workers and psychologists became involved in this form of treatment.

Brief psychotherapy has its roots in psychoanalytic theory but differs from psychoanalysis in terms of goals and other factors. It is limited to removing or alleviating specific symptoms when possible. Intervention may lead to some reconstruction of personality, although it is not considered as the primary goal. As in more traditional forms of psychotherapy, the therapy must be guided by an orderly series of concepts directed toward beneficial change in the patient. It is concerned with the degree of abatement of the symptoms presented and the return to or maintenance of the individual's ability to function adequately. To attain this goal the individual may choose to involve himself in a longer form of therapy. Another goal is assistance in preventing the development of deeper neurotic or psychotic symptoms after catastrophies or emergencies in life situations.

---

[5]Ibid., p. 155.

Free association, interpretation, and the analysis of transference are also used successfully in a modified manner. According to Bellak and Small (1965), free association is not a basic tool in short-term therapy. It may arise in response to a stimulus from the therapist. Interpretation is modified by the time limit and the immediacy of the problem. Although it may occur in brief psychotherapy, it is commonly used with medical or environmental types of intervention.

Bellak also believes that positive transference should be encouraged. It is crucial in brief therapy that the patient sees the therapist as being likeable, reliable, and understanding. The patient *must* believe that the therapist will be able to help him. This type of relationship is necessary if treatment goals are to be accomplished in a short period of time. This does not mean that negative transference feelings are to be ignored, but it does mean that these feelings are not analyzed in terms of defenses.

The therapist assumes a more active role than in the traditional methods. He avoids picking up trends not directly related to the presenting problem. The positive is accentuated, and the therapist presents himself as an interested, helpful person. The difficulties faced by the patient are circumscribed. The environmental position in which the patient finds himself is used by the therapist to help the patient evaluate the reality of his situation in an attempt to modify and change it. Productive behavior is encouraged.

Diagnostic evaluation is extremely important in short-term therapy. Its aim is to understand the symptoms and the patient dynamically and to formulate hypotheses that can be validated by the historical data. The result of the diagnosis will enable the therapist to decide which factors are most susceptible to change and to select the appropriate method of intervention. Part of the evaluation should be the degree of discrepancy or accord between the patient's fantasies and reality. His probable ability to tolerate past and future frustrations should also be considered; the adequacy of his past and present relationships is also pertinent. The question "Why do you come now?" must be asked and means not only "What is it that is going on in your life that distresses you?" but "What is it that you expect in the way of help?" It is reasonable to assume that a request for help is motivated by emotional necessities, both external and internal, which are meaningful to the patient. Short-term goals can be beneficial for *all* patients.

After determining the causes of the symptoms the therapist elects the appropriate intervention. Interpretation in order to achieve insight is used with care. Direct confrontation is used sparingly. An attempt is made to strengthen the ego by increasing the patient's self-esteem. One facet of this approach is to help the patient feel that he is on a level with the therapist and that he is no less worthwhile nor are his problems more unusual than those of others. This technique not only relieves the patient's anxiety but also facilitates communication between the patient and the therapist. Other basic procedures used include the following: catharsis, drive repression and restraint, reality testing, intellectualization, reassurance and support, counseling and guidance to move the patient along a line of behavior, and conjoint counseling.[6]

The ending of treatment is an important phase in brief therapy. The patient must be left with a positive transference and the feeling that he may return if the need arises. The learning which has taken place during therapy must be reinforced in order to encourage the patient to realize that he has begun to understand and solve his own problems. This has a preventive effect that will help the patient to recognize possible future problems.

As an adjunct, drug therapy may be used in selected cases. This is in contrast to pure psychoanalysis, where such is seldom utilized. Environmental manipulation is considered when it is necessary to remove or modify an element causing disruption in the patient's life pattern. Included might be close scrutiny of family and friends, his job and job training, education, plans for travel, and so forth.[7]

Brief psychotherapy is indicated in cases of acutely disruptive emotional pain, in cases of severely destructive circumstances, and in situations endangering the life of the patient or others. Another indication involves the life circumstances of the individual. If he cannot involve himself in the long-term therapeutic situation, which implies a stable residence, job, and so forth, brief therapy is advocated to alleviate disruptive symptoms.

It is imperative that the patient feel relief as rapidly as possible, even during the first therapeutic session. The span of treatment can be any reasonable, limited number of sessions but usually is from one to six. Most clinics expect the number of visits to be under twenty. Treatment goals can be attained in this short period of time if the patient is seen quickly and intensively after requesting help. Circumstances associated with disrupted functioning are more easily accessible if they are recent. Only active conflicts are amenable to therapeutic intervention. Disequilibrated states are more easily resolved *before* they have crystallized, acquired secondary gain features, or developed into highly maladaptive behavior patterns.

CRISIS INTERVENTION

Crisis intervention extends logically from brief psychotherapy. The minimum therapeutic goal of crisis intervention is psychological resolution of the individual's immediate crisis and restoration to at least the level of functioning that existed prior to the crisis period. A maximum goal is improvement in functioning above the precrisis level.

Caplan emphasizes that crisis is characteristically self-limiting and lasts from four to six weeks. This constitutes a transitional period, representing both the

---

[6]Bellak, Leopold, and Small, Leonard: Emergency psychotherapy and brief psychotherapy, New York, 1965, Grune & Stratton, Inc., pp. 52-66.
[7]Op. cit., pp. 74-85.

danger of increased psychological vulnerability and an opportunity for personality growth. In any particular situation the outcome may depend to a significant degree upon the ready availability of appropriate help. On this basis the length of time for intervention is from four to six weeks, with the median being four weeks.[8]

Since time is at a premium, a therapeutic climate is generated that commands the concentrated attention of both therapist and patient. A goal-oriented sense of commitment develops in sharp contrast to the more modest pace of traditional treatment modes.

Methodology

Jacobson and associates[9] state that crisis intervention may be divided into two major categories, which may be designated as individual or generic. These two approaches are complementary.

Generic approach

A leading proposition of the generic approach is that there are certain recognized patterns of behavior in most crises. Many studies have substantiated this thesis. For example, Lindemann's (1944) studies of bereavement found that there is a well-defined process that a person goes through in adjusting to the death of a relative. He refers to these sequential phases as "grief work" and found that failure of a person to grieve appropriately or to complete the process of bereavement could potentially lead to future emotional illness.

Subsequent studies of generic patterns of response to stressful situations have been reported. Kaplan and Mason (1960)* and Caplan (1964)* studied the effect on the mother of the birth of a premature baby and identified four phases or tasks that she must work through to ensure healthy adaptation to the experience. Janis (1958)* suggests several hypotheses concerning the psychological stress of impending surgery and the patterns of emotional response that follow a diagnosis of chronicity. Rapoport (1963)* defines three subphrases of marriage, during which unusual stress could precipitate crises. These are only a few of the broad research studies being done in this field.

The generic approach focuses on the characteristic course of the *particular kind of crisis* rather than on the psychodynamics of each individual in crisis. A treatment plan is directed toward an adaptive resolution of the crisis. Specific intervention measures are designed to be effective for all members of a given group rather than for the unique differences of one individual. Recognition of these behavioral patterns is an important aspect of preventive mental health.

---

*These studies are also discussed in Chapters 6 and 7 of this text.

[8]Jacobson, Gerald: Crisis theory and treatment strategy; some sociocultural and psychodynamic considerations, J. Nerv. Ment. Dis. **141**:209-218, 1965.

[9]Jacobson, Gerald, Strickler, M., and Morley, Wilbur E.: Generic and individual approaches to crisis intervention, Am. J. Public Health **58**:339-342, 1968.

Tyhurst[10] has suggested that knowledge of patterned behaviors in transitional states occurring during intense or sudden change from one life situation to another might provide an empirical basis for the management of these states and the prevention of subsequent mental illness. He cites as examples the studies of individual responses to community disaster, migration, and retirement of pensioners.

Jacobson and associates[11] state that generic approaches to crisis intervention include "direct encouragement of adaptive behavior, general support, environmental manipulation and anticipatory guidance. . . . In brief, the generic approach emphasizes (1) specific situational and maturational events occurring to significant population groups, (2) intervention oriented to crisis related to these specific events, and (3) intervention carried out by non-mental health professionals."

This approach has been found to be a feasible mode of intervention that can be learned and implemented by nonpsychiatric physicians, nurses, social workers, and so forth. It does not require a mastery of knowledge of the intrapsychic and interpersonal processes of an individual in crisis.

Individual approach

The individual approach differs from the generic in its emphasis on assessment, by a professional, of the interpersonal and intrapsychic processes of the person in crisis. It is used in selected cases, usually those not responding to the generic approach. Intervention is planned to meet the unique needs of the individual in crisis and to reach a solution for the particular situation and circumstances that precipitated the crisis. This differs from the generic approach, which focuses on the characteristic course of a particular kind of crisis.

Unlike extended psychotherapy, there is relatively little concern with the developmental past of the individual. Information from this source is seen as relevant only for the clues that may result in a better understanding of the present crisis situation. Emphasis is placed on the immediate causes for disturbed equilibrium and on the processes necessary for regaining a precrisis or higher level of functioning. Jacobson cites the inclusion of family members or other important persons in the process of the individual's crisis resolution as another area of differentiation from most individual psychotherapy.

In comparison with the generic approach he views the individual approach as emphasizing the need for greater depth of understanding of the biopsychosocial process, intervention oriented to the individual's unique situation and carried out only by mental health professionals.

---

[10]Tyhurst, J. A.: Role of transition states—including disasters—in mental illness, Symposium on Preventive and Social Psychiatry sponsored by Walter Reed Army Institute of Research, Walter Reed Medical Center, and National Research Council, April 15-17, 1957, Washington, D. C., 1957, U. S. Government Printing Office, pp. 149-172.
[11]Jacobson, Strickler, and Morley: Generic and individual approaches to crisis intervention, pp. 339-342.

Morley and co-workers[12] recommend several attitudes that are important adjuncts to the specific techniques. In essence these comprise the general philosophical orientation necessary for the full effectiveness of the therapist.

1. It is essential that the therapist view the work that he is doing not as a "second-best" approach but as the treatment of choice with persons in crisis.

2. Accurate assessment of the presenting problem, *not* a thorough diagnostic evaluation, is essential to an effective intervention.

3. Both the therapist and the individual should keep in mind throughout the contacts that the treatment is sharply time limited and should persistently direct their energies toward resolution of the presenting problem.

4. Dealing with material not directly related to the crisis has no place in an intervention of this kind.

5. The therapist must be willing to take an active and sometimes directive role in the intervention. The relatively slow-paced approach of more traditional treatment is inappropriate in this type of therapy.

6. Maximum flexibility of approach is encouraged. Such diverse techniques as serving as a resource person or information giver, taking an active role in established liaison with other helping resources, and so forth are often appropriate in particular situations.

7. The goal toward which the therapist is striving is explicit. His energy is directed entirely toward returning the individual to at least his precrisis level of functioning.

Steps in crisis intervention

There are certain specific steps[13] involved in the technique of crisis intervention. Although each cannot be placed in a clearly defined category, typical intervention would pass through the following sequence of phases:

1. The first phase is the assessment of the individual and his problem. This requires the use of active focusing techniques on the part of the therapist to obtain an accurate assessment of the precipitating event and the resulting crisis that brought the individual to seek professional help. The therapist may have to judge whether the help-seeking person presents a high suicidal or homicidal risk. If the patient is thought to be a high level of danger to himself or to others, referral is made to a psychiatrist for consideration of hospitalization. In the event that hospitalization is not deemed necessary, the intervention proceeds.

The initial hour may be spent entirely on assessing the circumstances directly relating to the immediate crisis situation.

2. Planning of therapeutic intervention: After accurate assessment is made of

---

[12]Morley, Wilbur E., Messick, Janice M., and Aguilera, Donna C.: Crisis; paradigms of intervention, J. Psychiatr. Nurs. **5:**537-538, 1967.

[13]Morley, Messick, and Aguilera: Crisis; paradigms of intervention, pp. 538-540.

the precipitating event(s) and the crisis, intervention is planned. This is not designed to bring about major changes in the personality structure but to restore the person to at least his precrisis level of equilibrium. In this phase, determination is made of the length of time since onset of the crisis. The precipitating event usually occurs from one to two weeks before the individual seeks help. Frequently it may have occurred within the past twenty-four hours. It is important to know how much the crisis has disrupted the individual's life and the effects of this disruption on others in his environment. Information is also sought to determine what strengths the individual has, what coping skills he may have used successfully in the past and is not using presently, and what other people in his life might be used as supports for him. Search is made for alternative methods of coping that for some reason he is not presently using.

3.   Intervention: The nature of intervention techniques is highly dependent on the preexisting skills, creativity, and flexibility of the therapist. Morley suggests some of the following, which have been found useful:

    a. *Helping the individual to gain an intellectual understanding of his crisis.* Often the individual sees no relationship between a hazardous situation occurring in life and the extreme discomfort of disequilibrium that he is experiencing. The therapist could use a direct approach, describing to the patient the relationship between crisis and the event in his life.

    b. *Helping the individual bring into the open his present feelings to which he may not have access.* Frequently the person may have suppressed some of his very real feelings such as anger or other inadmissible emotions toward someone he "should love or honor." It may also be denial of grief, feelings of guilt, or incompletion of the mourning process following bereavement. An immediate goal of intervention is the reduction of tension by providing means for the individual to recognize these feelings and bring them into the open. It is sometimes necessary to produce emotional catharsis and reduce immobilizing tension.

    c. *Exploration of coping mechanisms.* This approach requires assisting the person to examine alternate ways of coping. If for some reason the behaviors he used in the past for successfully reducing anxiety have not been tried, the possibility of their use in the present situation is explored. New coping methods are sought, and frequently the person devises some highly original methods that he has never tried before.

    d. *Reopening the social world.* If the crisis has been precipitated by the loss of someone significant to the individual's life, the possibility of introducing new people to fill the void can be highly effective. It is particularly effective if supports and gratifications provided by the "lost" person in the past can be achieved to a similar degree from the new relationships.

4.   The last phase is the resolution of the crisis and anticipatory planning. The

therapist reinforces those adaptive coping mechanisms that the individual has used successfully to reduce tension and anxiety. As his coping abilities increase and positive changes occur, they may be summarized to allow him to reexperience and reconfirm for himself the progress he has made. Assistance is given as needed in making realistic plans for the future, and there is discussion of ways in which the present experience may help in coping with future crises.

SUMMARY

A differentiation between psychoanalysis, brief psychotherapy, and crisis intervention methodology has been explored. No attempt has been made to state that one type of therapy is superior to another. In Table 1 we have provided the reader with a succinct profile of some of their major differences.

In psychoanalysis the goal of therapy is that of restructuring the personality; the focus of treatment is on the genetic past and the freeing of the unconscious. Psychoanalytic psychotherapeutic procedures are usually divided into two functional categories: the supportive (suppressive) and uncovering (exploratory or expressive) procedures. The therapist's role is nondirective, exploratory, and that of a passive observer. Indications for this type of therapy are for those individuals with neurotic personality patterns. Length of the therapy is indefinite and depends on the individual and the therapist.

Brief psychotherapy has as its goals removing specific symptoms and aiding in the prevention of developing deeper neurotic or psychotic symptoms. Its focus is

Table 1. Major differences between psychoanalysis, brief psychotherapy, and crisis intervention methodology

	Psychoanalysis	*Brief psychotherapy*	*Crisis intervention*
Goals of therapy	Restructuring the personality	Removal of specific symptoms	Resolution of immediate crisis
Focus of treatment	1. Genetic past	1. Genetic past as it relates to present situation	1. Genetic present
	2. Freeing the unconscious	2. Repression of unconscious and restraining of drives	2. Restoration to level of functioning prior to crisis
Usual activity of therapist	1. Exploratory	1. Suppressive	1. Suppressive
	2. Passive observer	2. Participant observer	2. Active participant
	3. Nondirective	3. Indirect	3. Direct
Indications	Neurotic personality patterns	Acutely disruptive emotional pain and severely disruptive circumstances	Sudden loss of ability to cope with a life situation
Average length of treatment	Indefinite	From one to twenty sessions	From one to six sessions

on the genetic past as it relates to the present situation, repression of the unconscious, and restraining of drives. The role of the therapist is indirect, suppressive, and that of a participant observer. Basic tools used are psychodynamic intervention coupled with medical or environmental types of intervention. Indications for brief psychotherapy are acutely disruptive emotional pain, severely disruptive circumstances, and situations endangering the life of the individual or others. It is also indicated for those who have problems that do not require psychoanalytic intervention. The average length of treatment is from one to twenty sessions.

The goal of crisis intervention is the resolution of an immediate crisis. Its focus is on the genetic present, with the restoration of the individual to his precrisis level of functioning or possibly to a higher level of functioning. The therapist's role is direct, suppressive, and that of an active participant. Techniques are varied and limited only by the flexibility and creativity of the therapist. Some of these techniques follow: helping the individual gain an intellectual understanding of his crisis, assisting the individual in bringing his feelings into the open, exploring past and present coping mechanisms, finding and using situational supports, and anticipatory planning with the individual to reduce the possibility of future crises. The indications for this type of therapy are an individual's (or family's) sudden loss of ability to cope with a life situation. The average length of treatment is from one to six sessions.

REFERENCES

Alexander, Franz: Psychoanalysis and psychotherapy, New York, 1956, W. W. Norton & Co., Inc.

Bellak, Leopold, and Small, Leonard: Emergency psychotherapy and brief psychotherapy, New York, 1965, Grune & Stratton, Inc.

Caplan, Gerald: Principles of preventive psychiatry, New York, 1964, Basic Books, Inc., Publishers.

Freud, Sigmund: Collected papers. Translated by Joan Riviere and Alex and James Strachey; London, 1924, Hogarth Press, vol. 1.

Janis, Irving L.: Psychological stress; psychoanalytical and behavioral studies of surgical patients, New York, 1958, John Wiley & Sons, Inc.

Kaplan, D. M., and Mason, E. A.: Maternal reactions to premature birth viewed as an acute emotional disorder, Am. J. Orthopsychiatry **30:**539-552, 1960.

Lindemann, Erich: Symptomatology and management of acute grief, Am. J. Psychiatry **101:**101-148, Sept. 1944.

Mason, E. A.: Method of predicting crisis outcome for mothers of premature babies, Public Health Rep. **78:**1031-1035, 1963.

Rapoport, Rhona: Normal crises, family structure, and mental health, Family Process **2:**68-80, 1963.

Tarachow, Sidney: An introduction to psychotherapy, New York, 1963, International Universities Press.

ADDITIONAL READINGS

Brandon, S.: Theory and possibilities of therapeutic intervention, Br. J. Psychiatry **117:**627-633, Dec. 1970.

Caplan, Gerald: Emotional crisis. In Deutsch, A., and Fishbein, H., editors: The encyclopedia of mental health, vol. 2, New York, 1963, Franklin Watts, Inc.

Caplan, Gerald, and Grunebaum, H.: Perspectives on primary prevention, Arch. Gen. Psychiatry **17:**331-346, Sept. 1967.

Decker, J. B., and Stubblebine, J. M.: Crisis intervention and prevention of psychiatric disability; a follow-up study, Am. J. Psychiatry **129:**725-729, Dec. 1972.

Dressler, D. M., and Nash, K. B.: An approach to crisis intervention through team expansion, Am. J. Orthopsychiatry **42**(2): 317, 1972.

Ford, Donald H., and Urban, Hugh B.: Systems of psychotherapy, New York, 1963, John Wiley & Sons, Inc.

Fromm-Reichmann, Frieda: Psychoanalysis and psychotherapy, Chicago, 1959, The University of Chicago Press.

Hankoff, L. D.: Emergency psychiatric treatment, Springfield, Ill., 1968, Charles C Thomas, Publisher.

Langsley, Donald G., and Kaplan, David M.: The treatment of families in crisis, New York, 1968, Grune & Stratton, Inc.

Rapaport, Lydia: The state of crisis; some theoretical considerations, Chicago, 1972, The University of Chicago Press.

Raphael, Beverly: Crisis intervention; theoretical and methodological considerations, Aust. N. Z. J. Psychiatry **5**:183-190, 1971.

3 Group therapy concepts in crisis intervention

GROUP CONCEPTS

From birth on, the individual is a member of a group composed of himself and his parents. His life becomes a succession of group memberships, expanding from the basic family unit to peer groups, play groups, and groups in school, business, and church. An individual may remain in some groups permanently or temporarily, voluntarily or involuntarily, and in some directly or indirectly, but he will usually participate in some form of group activity until death.

A helpless infant depending upon the actions of others for survival progresses through intellectual, emotional, and social development. Forms of behavior that communicate feelings, needs, and ideas develop through interactions with others. At the same time, perceptions and reactions toward the feelings, needs, and ideas of others develop.

It has been suggested (Asch, 1951; Merton, 1961) that an individual's behavior can be controlled and influenced by the forces of groups of which he is a member and that he becomes what he is because of the roles, status, and functions that are taken or given in them. Interpersonal skills are neither inherited nor instinctive but are acquired through a continual learning process involving use of all the senses. Facial expressions, vocal tones, body movements, odors, touch, and so forth are all a part of the language of interpersonal communications. Since man communicates through nonverbal as well as verbal clues, deprivation of any one of the senses could lead to distorted perceptions of the actions and responses of others.

Experiences that bring feelings of comfort and satisfaction are usually tried again, whereas those that result in frustration and discomfort are avoided whenever possible so that progressive learning is based on past experiences. If a child's first important group, the immediate family, fails to provide him with gratifying, positive interpersonal learning experiences, his future psychosocial development could be impaired. For example, the child who has never learned how to obtain gratifying feelings of approval from within his family may be less than secure in establishing relationships with authority figures in other groups later, such as a teacher-pupil relationship in school. He may also experience added difficulties in his early peer groups, where beginning competition and leadership skills are first learned.

In recent years practical and scientific knowledge has been synthesized to form new concepts about the manipulation of group structures and group processes to effect change, both upon the group and upon its individual members. In psychiatry there has been a shift of emphasis from considering man as a biological entity to considering him as a biosocial entity. Movement has been increasingly away from an organism-centered to a social-centered conceptualization of personality dynamics. Other professions and social institutions have also been increasingly aware of the effects of group influences upon the individual.

During and immediately after World War II there was an increased recognition of the necessity to meet the special needs of groups of people for whom individual care was impossible. This contributed to a rapid rise in the development and acceptance of group therapy and other therapeutic groups in the military, veterans hospitals, and state and private institutions and clinics. Since then, an increasing variety of therapy groups has been developed in community and institutional settings, not only for patients with psychiatric problems but also for people unable to cope with many situational and maturational problems and stresses in daily life.

THERAPY GROUPS

Any simple definition of the term group therapy would be difficult because of a wide variety of concepts, methods, and interpretations of its meaning. In reference to people a group means, primarily, more than one person. If combined with the word therapy, it could mean, simply, a treatment given simultaneously to more than one person. When the group goal of effecting a change is included, it becomes more complicated because consideration must then be given to the methods and processes of group action, of individual action, and of the wide differences in group accomplishments.

Corsini and Rosenberg (1955) proposed a classification of group therapies in terms of involvement of intellectual, emotional, or action factors. Luchins (1964) suggests classifications based on concrete activities. According to Hinckley and Hermann (1951), one approach to understanding the differences between the many types of therapy groups has been to focus on their purposes and results. They suggest two main categories: *social group work* and *group therapy*.

Social group work

In social group work the purpose is to achieve a common group goal with the aid of a leader. A project or an activity is used to unite the members, and the chief result is socialization. Examples of this are recreational groups, calling for teamwork and sportsmanship, or rhythm and games groups; another example is sociodrama, in which symptomatic behavior is indirectly touched upon by participants through playacting. In this way discussions of feelings and behavior can be directed toward the *part* that is acted out, not toward the participant himself. Scouting and camping groups for children and adolescents are other means of fostering socialization and group-unifying activities.

In any of these social groups the leader serves as a director, discussant, or counselor. He must have skills in special areas, and his understanding of the dynamics of personality is secondary in importance to his understanding of group action and cultural patterns and mores. He is usually directive in his method of leading group activities along a prescribed course.

Slavson's (1964) approach to classifying therapy groups is to focus on the concept of depth in therapy for differentiating between types of psychotherapies. He acknowledges the concept of depth in therapy to be a controversial one, and there is apparently no absolute criterion for determining the absolute values of any one method in relation to another. The absence of accurate measuring devices makes it difficult to measure quantitatively changes in the psyche, functions, or attitudes resulting from therapy, and comparisons between methods could be misleading.

If the choice of method and course of psychotherapy is determined by the nature and intensity of individual needs, Slavson suggests a differentiation of psychotherapies based on the level of a person's psyche that requires change. Using this concept he has differentiated psychotherapy into the main categories of counseling, guidance, and psychotherapy.

Counseling

Counseling is reality oriented and focuses on solving specific problems arising from situational or interpersonal difficulties. The counselor is not required to be a trained psychotherapist but should have a greater knowledge than the counselee of the factors affecting the situation. His role is to direct actively toward the finding and acceptance of a solution to an immediate difficulty while not intentionally exposing the counselee's feelings or attitudes for the purpose of changing them. It is assumed that once the solutions are made clear, the ego will be able to function adequately toward solving the problem. The length of time in interviews is comparatively brief, and the sessions terminate as soon as the immediate specific difficulty is resolved. This method is least effective in group use.

Guidance

Guidance is a reality-oriented approach that may be used when a person finds himself incapable of coping with increased stresses because the emotional significance of a specific problem begins to affect his simple ego functioning. The aims and techniques are toward holding or reducing anxiety to a tolerable level and preventing disorganization. The focus is on correcting feelings and requires a professionally trained person with a sound understanding of psychodynamics and experience in psychotherapy that will enable him to work at this deeper level. The therapist's role is to supply clarification and support through empathy, acceptance, and permissiveness, thus enabling his client to bring conflictual feelings about the specific problem into conscious awareness and to ventilate them without increasing anxiety, guilt, or fear.

This approach may require a much longer period of time and more sessions than in the counseling approach because there is a need to prevent additional stress and discomfort, since the client is confronted with his feelings and he may be expected to change some of his perceptions, attitudes, and behaviors.

The use of groups appears to accelerate the guidance process, particularly when people with problems of a similar nature are brought together. There is mutual identification with the problem area, and interactions occur rapidly, members possibly providing each other with greater support of self-esteem through empathy, acceptance, and permissiveness than the therapist alone could provide. Negative feelings of being uniquely alone in needing help with a problem are alleviated.

Guidance has been found particularly effective in dealing with adolescents, persons with marital problems, families, parents of handicapped children, and so on. The therapist's role in the group requires him to be able to use skills necessary for psychotherapy, recognizing and avoiding threatening areas for each member while working with the group as a whole. Feelings and behaviors are explored only as they are significant to the reality of each member's life situation; unrestricted exploration of feelings is avoided.

Group psychotherapy

Group psychotherapy is intended to make fundamental personality changes and to investigate reasons for personal emotional problems (Hinckley and Hermann, 1951). Unlike counseling or guidance it does not aim to solve a single specific situational problem; rather, it aims toward correction of intrapsychic processes that will make the person more capable of dealing with many problems.

The group approach is based on concepts of individual psychotherapy. Free association and unrestricted exploration of emotions are encouraged. Unlike social or guidance groups there is no one specific group goal, and each member has his own specific aims and expectations as to what the group experience can offer. Cohesiveness of members develops from the stresses and pain they experience as they focus on emotional problems, traumatic memories, and uncovered feelings, and possibly from mutual identification with any specific reality problem area. Efforts to minimize these feelings by resorting to gamelike activities are not permitted. Rather than avoiding threatening areas, the therapist takes relatively few precautions and encourages ventilation or catharsis of feelings. General therapeutic goals for patients with functional illness are to relieve tensions and anxiety, help them to gain some insights into their problems, assist them to resolve some of their conflicts, and support them in replacing or changing maladaptive behaviors for adaptive ones.

Group therapy utilizes a variety of techniques to obtain its general aims, and therapists often differ in their leadership roles. Some actively direct, whereas others may deem it more therapeutic to take a passive, indirect role to a degree that the group appears to be self-directed.

Although there is a relationship between technique and theory, few present-day techniques have been derived *solely* from theory. The therapist will undoubtedly be testing out certain theories and hypotheses of psychodynamics and group dynamics; this is an intrinsic part of his professional-scientific role. At the same time, he also has the role of "healer," assuming responsibilities to help individuals solve concrete problems encountered in their daily living.

Some therapists may focus on the psychodynamics of individual behavior; others may focus on group dynamics. Sometimes the focus will remain on a theoretical, intellectual level rather than on the specific individual behavioral responses taking place within the immediate interactions of the group; more often than not there is a combination of both going on, and no one method can be criticized as being better or worse than another.

A most important responsibility for the therapist is interpreting to his patients the purpose for bringing the group together and the principles or rules under which they will operate. The patient's acceptance of this mode of therapy is determined in large part by whether he sees it as meeting his needs and whether he will be able to function under the principles of the group's operation. For example, the basic difficulties of a person may stem from early negative experiences in his primary family, and resultant avoidance reactions to group contacts could further increase his anxieties. Not only might this lead to increasing areas of conflict but the necessary positive transference phenomena would be unlikely. Selection criteria for members vary widely according to their needs, the availability and special areas of expertise of qualified therapists, and the purpose of the groups. These factors may also influence the size of membership, and there is no general agreement as to the number of sessions needed to accomplish specific goals.

The group process provides more than one person with whom the individual may identify and test out reactions to past experiences. In addition to the parental role figure that the therapist is most likely to be seen as, there are the sibling role figures of other members with whom interactions take place. In this way it provides on a small scale a situation in which a problem in interpersonal relationships can be exposed, a setting for action, reaction, and interaction within a therapeutic environment, and distorted perceptions of interpersonal experiences in the past can be revealed and examined. Varied interpersonal stimuli will be received from more than one source, and increasing opportunities for transference phenomena to take place and to be worked through will occur. Briefly, a transference phenomenon occurs when a person reacts to someone in the present as he did to someone in the past. This is because there is a tendency in everyone to carry over, into the present, attitudes and impressions gained from past interpersonal experiences. Although the present person may possess only one or two of the characteristics of the past person, a generalized distortion of the relationship can be triggered off. He becomes the recipient of the emotional responses and reactive behaviors that, in reality, were learned in the past relationship.

One therapeutic goal is to modify and clarify feelings, and feelings must be labeled and then verbalized in order for this to take place. The group provides an incentive in this area by open discussion during which patients are stimulated by the fact of emotions expressed by others and by the opportunity to relate their own problems to others in the group. Changed or new behavior responses can be tried out, observed in action, reflected back, and the dynamics explored for cause-and-effect reactions. Providing opportunities to increase coping capacities is important because this reflects the ability to resolve emotional issues and interpersonal problems that create conflicts.

For the individual, group experience is primarily an emotional one, and through interactions with other members he is confronted by relationships that may be supportive, critical, or a combination of both. Members are encouraged to both criticize and support each other, support occurring most often through mutual acceptance and empathic responses from other members. The presence of others is perceived as a protection against being the only object of the therapist's attention. Acceptance by a peer group rather than by just one person, the therapist, is reassuring, and feelings of being different and isolated are counteracted by the discovery that these same feelings and problems may be shared by others. It seems generally agreed that intergroup support is essential to the growth of a therapy group. Group interaction should assist the members to achieve insight into past behavior and to gain self-awareness in learning to adapt to more positive and satisfying interpersonal experiences in the future.

CRISIS GROUPS

Since the term group therapy may mean any two individuals who are in therapy together with a therapist, certain terms that may be unfamiliar to those who have not been involved in conducting therapy will be clarified. When *individual* crisis intervention therapy is mentioned, it means that an individual is in therapy on a one-to-one relationship with the therapist (Case study: Status and role change, Chapter 6, p. 74). *Conjoint* therapy refers to therapy that is conducted with a husband and wife who are seen by the therapist together (Case study: Prematurity, Chapter 6, p. 69). *Family* therapy includes those members of the family who are involved or affected by the crisis situation (Case study: Prepuberty, Chapter 7, p. 111). *Collateral* therapy could include almost any combination of two individuals who are involved in the crisis: mother-son, father-son, mother-daughter, father-daughter, boyfriend-girlfriend, boyfriend-boyfriend, roommates, and so forth. (Case study: Young adulthood, Chapter 7, p. 121). The term crisis *group* refers to a collection of individuals who are unknown and unrelated to each other who meet as a group with a therapist to work together toward resolution of their individual crises through group interaction (Case study: Mrs. L., Chapter 3, p. 35).

Treatment goals

The goal of a crisis group is that of returning the individual members of the group to at least their precrisis level of functioning and possibly to a higher level with an increased ability in problem solving. The focus of treatment (like that of crisis intervention individual therapy) is orientated to the present and to the problem that is of concern at the time the individuals request help. It deals with the stresses and balancing factors that are either absent or ineffective in the present crisis situation and is directed toward assisting the members to achieve a resolution of their crises. With the therapist the members explore the crisis-precipitating events, the crisis, past coping skills (what they usually do when they cannot handle anxiety, tension, and so on), situational supports (whom they usually turn to for help), and what is going on at the present time that is preventing them from solving their problems. The group members quickly become a cohesive group, actively involved in helping other members develop new coping skills and find situational supports. The therapist keeps them aware that the number of sessions is limited to six, using such methods as reminding them that a certain member has only two more sessions left.

Selection of participants

The determination of whether individuals requesting help in a crisis situation would benefit more from group therapy sessions than from individual therapy sessions is initially left to the discretion of the intake worker who sees the patient first. It might be that a group is being formed or that an ongoing group is oriented toward problems similar to the one in which the individual is involved. For example, there may be groups of married couples experiencing marital discord, parents with problems that involve their children, a group whose members are trying to break the drug habit, and adolescents with problems (family, drugs, juvenile authority, and so forth). Another consideration is whether another member can be added to the group. The crisis groups are open ended—its members enter and leave at different times; some will be beginning in the group, others will be halfway through, and others will be terminating. Five to eight members is usually considered the best size for a crisis group; it can fluctuate weekly as some members are absent or are terminated and new members are added. The therapist who conducts the group can control this by limiting the number of intake interviews he schedules each week.

Other crisis groups have differing rather than common problems as their focus. The purpose of including individuals in one of these groups would be because the interviewer believes that the individual would benefit more by interaction in a group than in a one-to-one relationship with a therapist. It may be decided that part of his problem is due to inadequate interpersonal relations. The individual may be a social isolate by choice or by necessity, and his problem may be that he has never been able to establish satisfactory relationships with others because of low self-esteem, poor self-concept, or a real or imagined handicap; or he may be new to the area, functioning in a new job or school and having difficulty meeting and making friends and would benefit from a group experience. This also could be true with individuals who, although they might resist accepting the "advice of experts," would be more agreeable to changing faulty coping skills through group pressure.

If it is thought that a person would benefit from group therapy, he is told the time and day the group meets and is asked if he would be willing to participate. If he agrees, he is given an appointment for a pregroup interview with the therapist who will be conducting the group. In this interview the therapist assesses the individual and makes the final decision of recommending group or individual therapy. He determines the stressful event(s) that precipitated the crisis, the symptoms that are present, and the degree of disruption that the crisis is creating in the individual's life. If group therapy is the choice of treatment, the therapist discusses the format of the sessions. He explains the time element (six weekly sessions that last for one and one half to two hours), the necessity for focus on immediate problems, and the fact that some members will be new to the group and others will be terminating. If the group comprises members with a common problem area, he may briefly explain who is in the group; for example: Mr. and Mrs. X. who have been married for four years and are having problems in their marriage similar to those of other members. This technique assists those seeking help to relax and feel that their problem is not unique, that they are not alone, and that they can expect other members of the group to understand and help them reach a solution to their problem.

Format of sessions

The format of sessions is highly individual, not only with the therapist but also with the physical environment or setting where the group sessions meet. Members may be asked to wait in a reception room until the scheduled hour before bringing them into the office (or room) that has been assigned. Again, depending upon the therapist and the facility, a room may be set aside, the members going directly to the room and, in some cases, "starting" the session informally before the therapist arrives.

In the first part of the group session the therapist very briefly introduces new members and asks them to tell the reason why they came for help. The other members then tell the reason why they are there and will usually add at what stage they are in therapy and what they believe is being accomplished in the group.

Role of the therapist

The role of the therapist is active and direct. He functions as a participant leader in the group sessions, assisting the members to focus on the problem areas under discussion by restricting and diverting general social conversation and lengthy discussions of past occurrences that have no relevance to the present crisis of the individuals in the group. He also acts as a group facilitator and must be alert to the quiet, passive members and encourage their participation. Conversely, he must control and direct those highly verbal and dominant members without completely silencing them as participants. The therapist must be skillful in understanding and acting on nonverbal clues from the members of the group. An example of this was the silent wife who appeared to the group to be calm and unruffled while her verbal, aggressive husband in an angry tirade told the rest of the group about the problems he was having with their son who never talked to him, refused to mind, was never home, and so on. The therapist, observing the wife's nonverbal behavior (tense posture, hands folding her handkerchief over and over, lips tightly compressed—as if she did not dare to speak), interrupted the husband politely but firmly and asked the wife directly if this was the way their son acted toward his father. The wife looked at the rest of the group; they encouraged her, saying that she should know her son better than his father because she was with him more. Thus encouraged by the therapist and the group, she replied that their son did act this way toward his father and she believed that he had every reason to because he had no respect for him. Turning to her husband she said, "Why should he? Every time he sees you you are either drunk or mad at something and you are always fighting with him."

STUDIES OF CRISIS GROUPS

There is relatively little written about the effectiveness or ineffectiveness of crisis group therapy. Strickler and Allgeyer's[1] pilot study done at the Benjamin Rush Center in Los Angeles was one of the first to test the feasibility of conducting group therapy using the crisis intervention model. In this study, consideration was given to the unique role of the therapist, the dynamics of the group process, and the group instrument that was structured to lend itself to the characteristic phases of crisis resolution.

Selection of members and structure of the group were in most respects similar to the general admission procedures for individual crisis intervention. No one was eliminated from group therapy because of severe pathology. After the initiation of the pilot group, it was found necessary to eliminate the following two groups of individuals: (1) those whom the therapist believed were seriously suicidal or homicidal and in need of more concentrated and individualized attention; and (2)

---

[1]Strickler, M., and Allgeyer, J.: The crisis group; a new application of crisis theory, Social Work **12:**28-32, July 1967.

those who were unable to relate to others because of a psychotic state or who, because of a language barrier, were unable to communicate in English. In the intake interview the individual was allowed the opportunity of choosing individual therapy over group therapy if he so desired.

The study, which was conducted over a six-month period, served thirty patients and had an average weekly attendance of four to five sessions for each member. The size of the group in each session varied from four to eight members; five to six members each session were considered to be the optimum number for treatment purposes.

The crisis group at the Benjamin Rush Center was structured to correspond to the three sequential phases of crisis resolution. The first phase involved the formulation of the crisis situation for the patient, which was accomplished in the pregroup interview. The second phase constituted the utilization of the group to help the patient attempt to solve his problem. In the third phase the group reinforced and helped sustain the patient's confidence in his new way of coping.

A study by Morley and Brown[2] explored the disadvantages and advantages of crisis intervention groups. Their study was carried out at the Venice branch of the Benjamin Rush Center. This clinic serves those individuals who are usually underrepresented in most mental health facilities: families with an annual income of less than $4,000, blacks, those of Mexican or Spanish-American descent, or those whose main family wage earner is a blue-collar worker. The criteria for accepting individuals into the group were similar to those previously used by Strickler and Allgeyer.

Morley and Brown listed several advantages of crisis groups and individual crisis intervention not typically available in "traditional" group or individual psychotherapy. First, it brings help to a number of individuals in need of treatment who might be unwilling or unable to enter into traditional treatment. This would include individuals who are willing to accept help with a problem but who do not consider themselves in need of psychiatric treatment for a mental or emotional illness. Second, many individuals are unwilling to agree to long-term therapy but will accept help for a particular problem carried out over a short period of time. Third, the universality of crisis provides a common meeting ground between patient and therapist, and the terminology and concepts seem to be more understandable and more acceptable to many individuals.

It was concluded that there seemed to be some disadvantages that occurred in the crisis group approach when compared with a traditional group approach. First and primarily, the analysis of group process, which is a powerful tool in traditional group work, had to be sacrificed to a certain extent. The time-limited and problem-oriented crisis groups made it impossible to make as much use of process analysis

---

[2]Morley, W. E., and Brown, V. B.: The crisis-intervention group; a natural mating or a marriage of convenience? Psychother. Theory, Res. Prac. **6:**30-36, Winter 1968.

as with a longer-term group. The need to focus upon each individual's presenting problem limited dealing with group interaction on any but a superficial level. Second, there seemed to be some loss of spontaneity. It was often necessary for the therapist to use the technique of "going around" to be certain that all members became active participants as soon as possible. Third, there was some loss of continuity and a greater need for repetition. The members were constantly changing, and new members needed to be brought up to date on the problem areas of the other members. Finally, transference interpretation was minimized. Negative transference interpretation was minimized because there was not a long-term relationship to give the individuals support if there was a sharp focus upon strong negative feelings.

The study also compared crisis groups with individual crisis intervention. On the positive side, group support was apparent to a significant degree, and members of the group offered a considerable amount of help and assurance to particularly disturbed group members, both within and outside the group therapy session; significant social relationships often grew out of the group contacts, and group members were effective in suggesting alternate coping mechanisms to others in the group. The group provided an avenue for encouraging expression of feelings, and members who saw others in the group openly expressing their feelings were thus encouraged to express their own feelings.

On the negative side the primary problem was keeping each individual's crisis in sharp focus. With members presenting a wide variety of different crises, it was often difficult to keep each person dealing solely with the specific area necessary for successful resolution of the crisis. It was also difficult to identify the "correct crisis." In the second or third hour of therapy the original area identified as the crisis might be supplanted by another. In individual crisis therapy this could be reassessed and identified easier than in a group setting. Another problem area was that of destructive coping mechanisms offered by other members of the group. Because they did not understand the underlying dynamics operating within a particular individual, the suggestions they would make might be more maladaptive than adaptive. Morley and Brown believed that the group approach offered little or no saving of professional time. The pregroup interviews and cancellations seemed to have been of primary importance in producing this result.

One of the authors (Aguilera) also conducted crisis group therapy at this same center in Venice and concurs with the findings of Strickler and Allgeyer and those of Morley and Brown. The format of the sessions and admission to the group were essentially the same as those for the other studies cited, with one exception: The selection of members was made with a specific problem area in which to work. The problem area of the group was defined as those parents who were having problems with their young adolescents. These parents were seen in one group with the therapist, and their adolescent children were seen in another group with another therapist. The sessions usually lasted from one to one and a half hours and were scheduled concurrently for the same evening. There was close communication between therapists, usually immediately after a session. Occasionally it was decided that the parents and adolescents would benefit from a collateral session with both therapists present. This was usually scheduled either prior to or immediately following the group therapy session. These crises groups seemed extremely effective because of the specific focus on a problem area, and the interaction between the group members was exceptionally high. The members were able to support each other in decisions regarding their problems and to explore alternate ways of coping. During the intake interview and the pregroup interview the parent(s) and child were seen individually, and if necessary, together, to determine their reasons for requesting help, their willingness to enter a group, and the appropriateness of their membership in the group.

At the crisis center the young adolescents were soon referred to as the "Teenie-Bopper Group" and their parents as the "Parent Group." In order to present a brief overview of how group therapy functions using crisis-intervention techniques, a case study is presented to depict how the therapist and the group members interrelated in resolving their crisis.

It was initially believed by the intake worker that Mrs. L. would benefit more from group therapy (the Parent Group) than from individual therapy. She was by choice a social isolate and in all probability would resist efforts to modify her behavior with her daughter because she strongly believed that she was "right" and a "good mother." Cindy, in turn, would benefit from group therapy with those of her own age group (the Teenie Boppers) to gain their support or have her actions invalidated by them. They were scheduled for their pregroup interview with the therapist.

Case study

Mrs. L., 42 years of age and a grandmotherly appearing woman, came to a crisis intervention center for her pregroup interview with the therapist, accompanied by her 14-year-old daughter Cindy. Cindy and her mother had been referred to the center for therapy by juvenile authorities. Cindy had run away from home and had been picked up by the police while trying to hitchhike to a well-known "hippie" center in northern California. When Mrs. L. was notified that Cindy had been found and was at the police station, she refused to come down, stating to the officer, "You had better keep her; I can't do anything with her!" She was told to come to court the next morning.

Cindy was held overnight in a juvenile hall. This had apparently been a terrifying experience for her. She said that she had shared a room with two other girls but had been too frightened to sleep because they threatened to kill her if she "reported on their lesbian activities." She stated she would do anything to avoid going back to juvenile hall or a similar corrective institution.

Cindy was very attractive and mature socially as well as physically. She was quietly spoken and poised, was of above-average intelligence with A and B grades in school, and enjoyed tennis and playing the piano. She was well liked by her teachers but had few friends in her peer group.

Cindy told the therapist that she thought her mother's standards were too rigid and that she tried to keep her isolated from her own age group. She refused to let her participate in social activities or dating and would even wait for Cindy to get out of school and "walk" her home.

Mrs. L. said that Cindy had been a "good" girl until recently, very obedient, and so forth, and she could not understand her present behavior. When questioned about Cindy's father, Mrs. L. became quite angry and defensive and said they had been divorced for six years. She implied that she had "married beneath her" and that he drank too much and had difficulty in keeping jobs. It was the small amount of alimony and support for Cindy that had forced them to move from their original "middle-class" neighborhood to their present, low socioeconomic area. She was apparently attempting to isolate Cindy from the "undesirable elements and people" in the environment. She saw herself as a "good" mother who was trying to maintain middle-class morality while living among a lower class.

Group session

Phase I. Formulation of crisis situation. Mrs. L. was introduced to the other members of the group and asked by the therapist to state what problem she was having with Cindy. She repeated her previous remarks to the group about Cindy running away and what she had done and said to the officer. When asked what had preceded Cindy's running away (the precipitating event), she became quite verbal. She said Cindy had asked to go to a neighborhood teen social center where a dance was being held. Mrs. L. refused, feeling that "Cindy was too young . . . she would meet the 'wrong' kind of people . . . the events were not properly chaperoned, etc., etc." While Mrs. L. was watching television in the living room, Cindy sneaked out of the house, went to the dance, and got back without being found out. The next day a neighbor informed Mrs. L. that her daughter had seen Cindy at the dance.

Mrs. L. immediately went to school, had Cindy called out of class, and confronted her with the information. Cindy admitted she had attended the dance and that she would sneak out again if she got the chance. Mrs. L. slapped her, and Cindy ran from the school crying. When Cindy failed to come home that evening, Mrs. L. reported her missing to the police. Cindy was picked up the next afternoon. Mrs. L.'s previous method of coping, by denying the reality of the situation and by trying to isolate herself and Cindy from their environment, was no longer effective: Cindy was growing up and demanding more freedom and independence.

Group response. Some of the members of the group responded to Mrs. L.'s *comments* by making superficial supportive statements, such as, "It sure is difficult to raise kids these days!" and, "The kids must be acting this way because of the kind of world we live in." Others suggested that she was "too rigid," and, "You got to give the girl some freedom . . . she's not a baby anymore . . . you can't keep her a prisoner." Another offered alternate ways of coping: "You don't have to give in all the way, but give her a chance; if it doesn't work, then try something else." One member reminded her that her present behavior had *caused* Cindy to run away. Others challenged her with, "If you don't like the neighborhood, move; no one is keeping you there!" and, "If you don't have the money, go to work instead of staying home and playing the good mother."

Mrs. L.'s response to group. At first Mrs. L. reacted with hostility toward the group suggestions and confrontations. She still maintained her rigidity and saw her actions and behavior as justified. She rationalized them by stating firmly that she "couldn't care less what other people think," she knew she was right. Later, when the group members began making suggestions for different ways of maintaining discipline and still allowing Cindy some freedom, she responded with, "I'll consider it." She reacted warmly to those members who made supportive statements or suggestions and directed most of her remarks toward them. To the members who made negative statements she responded in an aloof, superior, cold manner and avoided conversation with them if she could.

Phase II. Intervention. In subsequent sessions Mrs. L. became more comfortable with the group members and felt less threatened. She began to adapt some of their suggestions in coping with Cindy. When the suggestions "worked," she always expressed her thanks to the member who had made the suggestion. She soon dropped her superior attitude toward group members and was able to express her feelings of guilt over slapping Cindy. She stated that she rarely had to punish Cindy because she was usually able to reason with her. She still maintained her "good mother" role in the group, and the group accepted her as an authority figure because she was very verbal and intelligent. They still challenged her rigidity and inconsistency about not wanting to work while Cindy was in school. She believed that she and her daughter were beginning to understand each other a little better.

The group members worked cohesively and sharply focused on specific problem areas. By the end of the third session they were interacting freely, testing new coping devices and reality testing within the group. Prior to the fourth group session the therapist had a pregroup interview with a Mr. G. His problems with his son appeared to be so similar to Mrs. L.'s that the therapist thought he would be a valuable addition to the group and would benefit from the group experience.

In the pregroup interview with the therapist Mr. G. expressed great concern over his son's changed behavior and appeared genuinely at a loss as to why he should now be presenting problems. He had also run away from home and had been picked up by authorities. He said he had tried hard to be a "good father" since his wife had left him five years ago, and he stated repeatedly how much he loved his son and what a good boy the son had always been prior to running away.

Mr. G. appeared to be a very mild-mannered man and was quiet almost to the point of shyness.

He entered the group at the fourth session. After being introduced he began talking about his son and his problems with him. Very matter-of-factly, with little emotional expression, he calmly stated: "I'm a good father, I love my son, I can't understand why he has changed. I've beaten the hell out of him since he was 5 years old, and with the buckle end of the belt half the time, and he still won't mind." The group members were shocked into silence. The therapist, recognizing this, remained silent to observe the responses of the individual members to this different attitude about disciplining a child.

Group response. The group recovered from their state of shock over Mr. G.'s announcement and immediately began to attack him verbally. Mrs. L. emerged as their "leader" in the attack. Their comments were personal and cutting. Mr. G. countered their attack by becoming hostile and just as verbally aggressive. It was obvious that the focus of the group was, at this time, shattered because the group had deviated from problem areas to attacking an individual's attitude and character. The therapist stopped the "debate" and confronted the group with their behavior. After a discussion period the group, at the insistence of the therapist, began to redirect the focus to problem areas of concern. Mrs. L., as the group leader, began to explain to Mr. G. how the group functioned and brought him up-to-date on the problems they had been working on together. Mr. G. remained mostly silent for the rest of the session, giving his opinion only if asked directly by a group member or the therapist.

(Therapist's note: Mr. G.'s attitude, and so on, in the pregroup interview was totally different from that displayed in the group. I was caught completely unaware by his change in behavior. It was a very valuable learning experience for the group *and* the therapist!)

Phase III. Termination. By the sixth session Mrs. L. had apparently resolved her crisis with the help of group support. She and Cindy were getting along well together. (This information was verified by Cindy and her therapist.) She admitted that occasionally minor problems occurred but that she and Cindy were usually able to reach an agreeable compromise. She became quite friendly with several members of the group. They even visited at each other's homes. Thus, Mrs. L. was able to overcome her illogical isolation of herself and Cindy from the low-income community. The most dramatic and encouraging change in behavior in Mrs. L. was apparent when she announced at the last session that, through the encouragment and help of another member, she had gotten a part-time job as a secretary at a local junior college. She had worked three days and, as she stated it, "I love it! I've never been happier and Cindy is so proud of me!"

It was at this session that the therapist and the group reviewed the progress and work they had done in the previous sessions to help Mrs. L. resolve her problem. Mrs. L. expressed some reluctance over terminating with the group. She was reassured by the members that they would "keep in touch." In an attempt to overcome her feeling of loss, Mrs. L. invited the entire group to her house for cake and coffee after the session. Everyone accepted the invitation.

SUMMARY

The behavior and personality of the individual may be changed by the forces of any group in which he is a member. Since World War II, the increasing awareness of the need to treat large groups of people has contributed to the rapid advances in the development and acceptance of group therapy and other therapeutic groups. An overview of therapeutic groups and group therapy has been presented to show the basis from which crisis groups evolved.

Since little has been written about crisis groups, two recent studies have been utilized for the purpose of showing their implementation, advantages, and disadvantages. A case study has been presented to demonstrate the use of crisis intervention techniques in a group therapy session.

REFERENCES

Asch, G.: Effects of group pressure upon the modification and distortion of judgment. In Guetzkow, H., editor: Groups, leadership and men, Pittsburgh, 1951, Carnegie Press, pp. 177-190.

Corsini, R. J., and Rosenberg, B.: Mechanisms of group psychotherapy, J. Abnorm. Social Psychol. **51:**406-411, 1955.

Hinckley, Robert G., and Hermann, Lydia: Group treatment in psychotherapy, Minneapolis, 1951, University of Minnesota Press.

Luchins, Abraham S.: Group therapy; a guide, New York, 1964, Random House, Inc.

Merton, Robert K.: Social theory and social structure, rev. ed., New York, 1961, The Free Press, Division of The Macmillan Co.

Slavson, S. R.: A textbook in analytic group psychotherapy, New York, 1964, International Universities Press.

ADDITIONAL READINGS

Allgeyer, Jean: The crisis group; its unique usefulness to the disadvantaged, Int. J. Group Psychother. **20:**235-240, April 1970.

Berns, E.: Principles of group treatment, New York, 1966, Oxford Book Co., Inc.

Bloch, H. Spencer: An open-ended crisis-oriented group for the poor who are sick, Arch. Gen. Psychiatry **18:**178-185, Feb. 1968.

Gazda, G. M., editor: Basic approaches to group psychotherapy and group counseling, Springfield, Ill., 1968, Charles C Thomas, Publisher.

MacGregor, R., and others: Multiple impact therapy with families, New York, 1964, McGraw-Hill Book Co.

Masserman, J., editor: Current psychiatric therapies, vol. 8, New York, 1968, Grune & Stratton, Inc.

Moreno, J. L., and others, editors: The international handbook of group psychotherapy, New York, 1966, Philosophical Library, Inc.

Pattison, E. M.: Group psychotherapy and group methods in community mental health programs, Int. J. Group Psychother. **20:**516-539, 1970.

Sater, Virginia M.: Conjoint family therapy, Palo Alto, Calif., 1964, Science & Behavior Books, Inc.

Slavson, S. R., editor: The fields of group psychotherapy, New York, 1966, John Wiley & Sons, Inc.

Small, Leonard: The briefer psychotherapies, New York, 1971, Brunner/Mazel, Inc.

4   Sociocultural factors affecting therapeutic intervention

In a discussion of some of the sociocultural factors than can act as barriers in the psychotherapeutic process there are two aspects to be considered. First, there are the professionals who are frustrated when trying to give help to someone from a different and unfamiliar sociocultural background; and second, there are those in need of help who are frustrated when they do not receive the kind of assistance they feel they need.

The following will not attempt to cover the gamut of specific ethnic and cultural factors present in today's society, but an effort will be made to discuss certain key areas that are usually considered to be problems and to help the reader become aware of the nature of these difficulties.

The inability to understand and accept the attitudes and values of those who are not in our same educational, economic, and ethnic group is a major barrier. Professionals are aware of its existence, since they experience difficulty and are uncomfortable when trying to communicate with those who do not share their same standards and ideas.

One reason for this is the sociocultural background of the professionals. The majority are from the dominant middle-class culture and have no difficulty in understanding and working comfortably with members of their own class culture. They speak the same language, have the same values ethically and morally, and share essentially the same expectations from life. When confronted with someone from a different sociocultural background seeking help, the professionals are frustrated in their desire to help because they may not understand what is being asked of them. Language and terminology are a mutual problem because codes of conduct and behavioral expectations are not always understood. Mutual suspicion is aroused, with the professional feeling that the individual does not really want his help, and the individual in need of help, not understanding what is expected of him, is uncomfortable and aggravates the situation of noncommunication.

Behavior and beliefs that are acceptable and highly valued in one cultural group may be unacceptable and devalued in another, or what is viewed as normal in one group could be abnormal in another.

Normal is the term society uses for social behaviors that are preferred, and *abnormal,* for those to which it objects (Benedict, 1934; Opler, 1956; Redlich, 1952). One of the big problems for social psychiatry is to determine just which feelings, thoughts, and actions are normal and which are abnormal. Who or what determines this? The term normal has several definitions. *Statistically* it can mean average, or the "norm." This is most likely to be seen in mathematical samples. When the term *adaptive* is used to mean normal behavior, it is more likely to be used psychiatrically. For example, normal behavior is the ability of the individual to adapt to ordinary environmental conditions without undue stress or anxiety. If the individual has more difficulty adapting to ordinary environmental conditions than the general group, his behavior could be labeled as being abnormal or mal-adaptive.

Benedict suggests that normality is culturally defined and cites as an example the behavior of the mystic who experiences trancelike states and catalepsy. In our general culture this would be considered abnormal behavior; in some cultures the greatest prestige is awarded to those who have trancelike experiences. They are considered blessed and are accorded the reverence due them as shaman in their communities. Their behavior is given cultural approval, and their roles as counselors and diviners are a necessary part of the social structure of their communities. It can be demonstrated in all cultures that honorable roles are assigned by society to those behaviors it needs and accepts, and devalued roles are assigned to those it no longer needs and rejects. From this frame of reference normality is defined by culture.

Consider the traditional Chinese culture, where the grandparents were revered by their descendants, bowed to, and given full obedience to their demands. Such expectations from grandparents in our culture would be considered abnormal. In some cultures suicide is considered to be a traditionally normal and honorable way to resolve problems. In our Western culture it is generally considered abnormal to the degree that there are laws against it, religious as well as societal, and any attempts are punishable as a crime against society. The same extremes of views among cultures are held toward such actions as homicide, homosexuality, and polygamy.

DIFFERING CULTURAL VALUES

Widely divergent cultural perceptions are also found between the values accorded family roles, child-rearing methods, and the roles and status given individuals relative to their age, sex, occupation, marital status, religion, education, and so forth. Changes vary with the conditions under which society must function. There are constant problems facing every culture in adapting to the environs and attempting to maintain cultural equilibrium. Most of their norms are directed toward their basic needs for survival (Opler, 1956).

It is important to avoid stereotyping if there is to be understanding and communication between members of different cultural classes. Preconceived ideas about who does what, and why it is done, are the strongest barriers to understanding behavior and effecting change.

An example of this is the traditional middle-class culture. It has been both attacked and supported in recent decades. Its values and ideals have been called the backbone of our society and the cause of our weaknesses. Both opinions probably hold elements of truth. Because of its pervasive influence upon all facets of our society it has been scrutinized, criticized, praised, and derogated. Today, many think it an insult to be accused of "middle-class thinking." Values and ideals that were once considered to be inviolate are now being challenged.

Traditional middle-class culture

Prior to the depression years of the 1930's the traditional middle-class ideals and values were based on the Protestant ethic—the idea that hard work and self-control would lead to success. Traditions of social behavior were strongly adhered to, with emphasis on self-discipline, individualism, and clearly defined roles in the family and community (Haas, 1963; Seward, 1956). Social stability was the key word.

This was the culture in which proverbs were lived, not hung on the walls as "pop-art" decorations. "Early to bed and early to rise makes a man healthy, wealthy, and wise" was a way of life. So, also, were "A stitch in time saves nine," "A rolling stone gathers no moss," "Virtue is its own reward," and the dozens of others that emphasized the goodness of industriousness, stability, and self-discipline, and the evils of laziness, instability, and lack of self-control.

The father was expected by society to reign unchallenged in his role as patriarch and breadwinner in his family. His wife obeyed him, and her role was relegated to the family, kitchen, and church. The children were expected to be obedient to both parents. Impulsive actions and aggressive hostility were frowned upon. Family roles were clearly defined and were reinforced by the social institutions of the times (Seward, 1956). Traditional education emphasized discipline, order, and authority. Christian morality still held the puritanical tenets of fear of God's judgment for any real or imagined sins against His teachings. Sex was only a three-letter word, not acceptable for use in mixed company or "polite" conversation.

This was the era of strong conscience and of fear of punishment and social disfavor if any deviance were discovered. Today it would be said that the middle-class culture of that era was ruled by overly severe superegos. These were a tradition-bound, hard-working people who were, in many ways, the necessary source of stability in the rapidly changing society in the United States. As progressive changes occurred in the overall society, cultural changes followed.

New middle-class culture

The values and ideals of any culture reflect the attitudes and needs of its society. With technological advances the United States has become increasingly industrialized and urbanized. The core of the "old" middle class decreased in numbers. The predominating cultural values and needs of the rural independent farmers and the small-town entrepreneurs were supplanted by the changing needs of the urban middle class (Riessman and Miller, 1964). The children no longer were expected to be the tradition bearers of their rural home communities. They moved on to less stable urban areas, and the old ideals, attitudes, and values failed to meet their changing needs. Industriousness no longer was a guarantee of personal success. Too often a man was working for someone else, and self-employment was the exception rather than the rule. Authoritarianism and self-control were coming into conflict with the changing values of an increasingly technological society. Creativity, individual autonomy, and self-expression grew in cultural value.

Child-rearing and educational goals reflect these changing ideals, attitudes, and values. Permissiveness and self-expression have gained in favor (Riessman and Miller, 1964). Individualism has given way to the concepts of group membership, cooperation, and teamwork. High value is placed on the individual's ability to interrelate with others. Cultural emphasis on these last factors is exemplified by the never-failing request for evaluations of a person's interpersonal and communication skills in reference questionnaires sent out by employers.

The "new" middle-class culture shows the effects of the vast changes introduced into American society since World War II. Yet it retains the basic high valuation of thrift, industriousness, and self-control, which still permeate the structure of its institutions. Socioeconomic stratification of classes has diffused these values into other sociocultural classes.

TRADITIONAL TREATMENT METHODS

Federal legislation has made increased funding available for the development of community programs and facilities. Professional disciplines have shifted the focus of their activities to include consideration of the sociocultural components of mental illness. The accumulation of data over the past decade suggests that there are several important factors that are considered barriers to effective therapeutic intervention. Until ways are found to overcome these barriers, successful programs will be limited in the scope of their activities.

One of the main criticisms of the traditional psychiatric treatment methods is that they have become self-limiting by the very nature of their origins. Theories and techniques have been developed by professionals who come predominantly from the middle class and identify with its cultural values and goals. For example, Freud's psychoanalytic theories were based on his observations made in a middle-class continental culture with a relatively stable environment (Seward, 1956). His norms were a reflection of the norms of his culture, and his therapy was focused toward adaptation to those norms. One of his basic assumptions was that a patient would have enough time and money to continue in a long course of private therapy sessions. A prevailing theme in literature is the dominant middle-class character of the mental health movement (Haas, 1963; Riessman and Scribner, 1965; Yamamoto and Goin, 1965).

A number of studies (Heine and Trossman, 1960; McMahon, 1964; Myers and associates, 1968) have attempted to identify the character traits of the patient who might be most likely to "succeed" in psychodynamic-based therapies. The consensus describes him as a person who feels a strong need to relate to people, particularly when he has problems. He is psychologically oriented, has the intellectual capacity to deal with abstracts, is sophisticated in the jargon of psychiatry, and has some idea of the values and goals of psychotherapy. This makes it easier for him to communicate his feelings to the therapist. A basis for mutual understanding is more readily established. He is introspective in nature and probably has a strong tendency to blame himself, rather than others, for his problems. He is highly motivated to find out why he feels the way he does and how he can change his life-style to make things better for himself. He places a high value on self-control and on his ability to accept delayed gratification of his needs, and he expects to have to put much of his own efforts into getting those needs met. For these reasons he accepts the lengthy time that he may have to spend in therapy and has positive feelings that it will be well worth his efforts. These characterological traits reflect many of the basic ones reported for the middle-class culture.

Until the early 1940's the main focus of treatment was derived from theories stressing the organic and psychological causes of mental illness. This was followed by a shift, which included the effects of interpersonal relationships on behavior and personality. Current emphasis on sociocultural factors influencing mental health has stimulated broad research in this area, particularly in the relatively new field of social psychiatry.

The basis of psychiatric treatment is the establishment of meaningful communication between the therapist and his patient. If he is unable to accomplish this, the therapist has few alternatives to offer. In order to establish a meaningful base of communication the therapist's responsibility is to have some awareness, if not a full understanding, of the needs, values, and goals of his patient.

Members of one socioeconomic class may not actually understand or be aware of the needs, values, and goals of another. As a result of the increasing number of mental health programs being maintained by state and local governments, more individuals from substandard sociocultural groups are having their first contacts with mental health professionals. At the same time, many of the mental health professionals are having *their* first contacts with these groups in their home environments. The appropriateness of treatment modalities is being questioned not only by the professionals but also by the public receiving them.

CLASS STRATIFICATION SYSTEMS

Since Hollingshead and Redlich (1958) completed their study of the relationships between social class and mental illness, further studies in the field have supported their findings (Albronda and associates, 1964; Brill and Storrow, 1960; Haas, 1963; Myers and associates, 1968). Relationships have been found to exist between social class and the development, type, prevalence, and treatment of mental illness. It appears that the lower a person's location is on the socioeconomic class scale, the more restricted is the range of available therapies.

Defining social classes might be done through either of two main approaches. The first, the *statistical* approach, can be drawn from the socioeconomic levels of education, income, occupation, and place of residence. This is most frequently seen in industrial- and government-type reports. Although this will convey a concrete differentiation between the American system of socioeconomic classes, it does not include any criteria for the sociocultural life styles of different groups of people. If only the statistical method is used, there may be a strong tendency to stereotype people into classes using only the available economic information about them. Poverty level in one part of the country might well be a comfortable lower middle-class level in another.

The second method of defining social classes, *life styles,* recognizes and accounts for the influences of the less well-defined, systematized behavior patterns, values, and life styles of groups of people, and their interrelated effects upon the socioeconomic classifications. In their study of a selected population group that was receiving psychiatric treatment, Hollingshead and Redlich (1958) utilized a classification format that took into consideration the values the subjects placed upon their education, income, occupation, and place of residence. They also developed a two-factor index (occupation and education) to determine social position. Occupation presumably reflected the skill and power that individuals possessed in society; education reflected not only knowledge but also cultural tastes. The proper combination of these two factors, using statistical techniques, enabled them to determine approximately the social position occupied by an individual in the structure of society.

In the collection and organization of their data they used a pattern of vertical divisions such as race, religion, and ethnic groupings. In addition they classified subjects in horizontal divisions according to their commonly held values attached to places of residence, occupations, educational backgrounds, and associations. This meant that, regardless of his race, religion, or ethnic grouping, an unskilled laborer with little formal education who lived in a poverty area of the community was ranked low in all of the vertical divisions' groupings.

Class I. This class consisted of the community's business and professional leaders. Its members lived in the best areas of the community; the men were college graduates, and their wives usually had completed from one to four years of college. Income was the highest of any class, and the members of the core group were descendants of the pioneers who settled in New England. The core group family was stable, secure, and socially responsible for its members and the welfare of the community. These families dominated the private clubs, and play was a prominent part of this group's use of leisure time.

Class II. Most of the adults in this class had some formal education beyond high school. The men occupied managerial positions, and many were engaged in lesser-ranking professions. Its members lived in one-family houses in the better residential areas. The families were well-to-do, but there was no inherited or acquired wealth. The nuclear family was composed predominantly of married adults and their minor children. They belonged to neighborhood clique groups, local church organizations, political clubs, and so on. Family members of all ages were "joiners."

Class III. The typical Class III man or woman was a high school graduate. The men were employees in various salaried positions: clerical, semiprofessional, or technical. The women also worked in clerical, sales, or technical positions. They tended to live in the "good" sections of the residential areas. The family included father, mother, and minor children but no other relatives or nonrelatives. Most members belonged to community organizations of one kind or another: fraternal orders, church clubs, athletic clubs, lodges, or veterans' groups. More men and women were dissatisfied with their present living conditions and less optimistic about the future than were those in Class II.

Class IV. The median years of school completed by the men was 9.4 years and by their wives, 10.5 years. The men were mostly semiskilled employees, skilled manual employees, or clerical and sales workers. Almost all of the women were working as semiskilled factory workers, clerical workers, or sales workers. The majority of the families lived in two-, three-, or multiple-family dwellings in the working-class sections of the city. The family income was spent, for the most part, as it was earned. The family constellation differed from that of Class III in four ways: There were more broken homes, more households had boarders and roomers, the families were larger, and there were more three-generation families living under one roof. Recreation consisted of "working around the place," watching television, listening to the radio, and family visiting. The husband belonged to the union but no other organization; the wife belonged to no formal organization but was a member of informal neighborhood women's groups.

Class V. This class had the poorest education in the population. The median years of school for men was six years and slightly less than eight years for the women. The men worked as semiskilled and unskilled workers, and some had never had a regular job. Jobs in this class were poorly paid, requiring long hours for six or seven days a week and in industries that were not unionized. Over two thirds of Class V persons lived in crowded tenement areas, the tenements housing from ten to fifty families. Family ties were more brittle in this class. Five types of families existed: the nuclear family of father, mother, and children; the three- or four-generation family; the broken nuclear residual families consisting of widows, widowers, or elderly couples; mixed families of one parent, children, and roomers; and the common-law groups. Only a small number of family members belonged to organized community institutions. Their social life took place in the household, on the street, or in neighborhood social agencies. Adults were resentful of the way they were treated by employers, clergymen, teachers, doctors, police, and other representatives of organized society.

An individual, for example, from Class IV or Class V could not invest the money nor the time for extensive psychotherapy. His education level would limit his understanding of the psychotherapeutic goals and terminology. He would be more concrete and direct in his thinking, and not particularly introspective. If he sought help, he would want it immediately, not six months from now. He is inclined to regard authorities with suspicion and dislike and will only seek their help as a last resort. In the follow-up study by Myers and associates (1968), individuals in Class V of the Hollingshead and Redlich study were the ones who had remained institutionalized and usually ended up dying there or had repeated admissions. This validates their suspicions that they should not ask for help unless absolutely forced to because the only help available to them is in institutions.

LOWER SOCIOCULTURAL GROUPS

Current literature puts various labels on the lower sociocultural groups. These are, for the most part, indications of the specific areas within the lower-class structure being studied. Designations have been made such as the "underprivileged," the "poor," the "culturally disadvantaged," the "culturally deprived," the "migratory worker," the "blue-collar worker," the "disenfranchised," ad infinitum. The one fact that they all seem to hold in agreement is that there are people who, for one reason or another, will always be found clustered at the lower level of any class-stratification system. A clear-cut criterion for just exactly "who" these people are has not been developed, and inconsistencies in results of studies of similar populations bear out this fact.

There are many scales of class measurement, and a person does not necessarily fall into all lower categories at the same time. Just because an individual is the unemployed head of a household and living on the fringes of a poverty area is no reason to categorize him with the culturally deprived. If this were so, there would be a large mass of college students eligible for cultural poverty programs! On the other hand, a blue-collar laborer making a good salary could feasibly be described as culturally deprived if there were a lack of cultural programs available to him.

Societies are usually structured around institutions that they have created to provide for the "normal" needs of their population. Judgments as to its "abnormal" needs are most often made by the same group that has determined the norms for their culture. Only in the recent history of the United States has there been active recognition of the high variability of cultural norms and values, and values of the dominant sociocultural class are no longer being left unchallenged as being "good" or "bad" for all of the society's members.

BARRIERS TO THERAPY

All of the groups (ethnic, racial, occupational, age, and so forth) who live in the culturally and economically lower margins of society have been categorized as "lower class." Much of the tone of literature about them tends to have a negative quality. In terms of socioeconomic programs there has always seemed to be more interest in what could be done for them rather than with them. This was particularly evident in programs to effect changes in their ways of life; little confidence was expressed in their ability to change. Only recently has there been emphasis on a new theme—that of recognizing their strengths rather than just their weaknesses and of going into their communities and working in a cooperative effort with them to make changes they *they* feel are most necessary.

Mental health professionals are well aware that the attitudes of the general community toward mental illness are a keystone in the development of any treatment program and that they should be recognized as determining the goals of the services offered. To be effective, a program should be meaningful and seen as needed by the community groups it is meant to reach.

Crisis intervention is by *no* means restricted to those of the lower sociocultural levels; however, because of certain inherent factors it is thought that its techniques are more effective for those at this level than are the techniques of other types of therapy.

Jacobson (1965) has stated that motivating forces have universal elements and precede cultural differences. Typically, people are wary of strangers, and time is needed to assess new situations and strangers in the environment. Under such circumstances they are usually guarded in their speech and controlled in their actions. In emergency situations such as fires, earthquakes, and other catastrophes, individuals work together freely, barriers to communication are lowered, and sociocultural levels are disregarded. This occurs similarly when a person is in a crisis and comes for help. The element of strangeness is quickly overcome as the individual and the therapist concentrate on relieving the symptoms of stress even though they may be from different sociocultural backgrounds.

The time-limiting factor of crisis intervention is a distinct advantage with those individuals in the lower sociocultural group, who are focused on the here and now and want relief of their symptoms as soon as possible. Crisis intervention is directed toward helping the individual solve a specific problem. Major characterological and behavioral changes are not expected, nor are they dwelt on in the therapy sessions. This lessens the threat to him because he does not have to expose his complete pattern of living, which may be different from that of the therapist.

A community mental health center conceivably serves individuals from different sociocultural levels. Psychotherapy for an extended period of time may be too expensive for an average middle-class family or person, and it may not be needed if a crisis situation exists. Those who may now be considered middle class may have originally come from a lower sociocultural background and may retain its views regarding the value of psychotherapy and misconceptions about mental illness.

Referrals to a community mental health center come from multiple sources. Family physicians may decide that certain individuals need help with an emotional problem and make the referral; attorneys, juvenile authorities, clergymen, family service agencies, and others may also make referrals. The community itself is usually aware through publicity (radio, newspapers, word-of-mouth, and liaison personnel) of a community center's function and the services available. Because of this publicity and location in the community they may serve many who "walk in" for help.

Conversely, referrals from a community mental health center are also diversified and are usually highly individualized. A person may be referred directly for hospitalization if dangerously suicidal or homicidal, for longer-term therapy after crisis intervention for chronic problems, to a family service agency if needed, or to a rehabilitation center.

The prevalent attitudes toward mental illness in our society are less than favorable. There is an aura of fear and anxiety surrounding overt mental disturbance. Much of this is due to the distorted ideas about what happens when a person "goes crazy" or "insane," which have been reinforced by the mass media (Tershakovek, 1964). Basic to many of the latest movies, television programs, or fiction that have been put out for the public are the elements of fear, loss of control, and questionable "recovery"—believable yet grossly exaggerated for impact and saleability.

The lower sociocultural groups, in particular, fear mental illness (Riessman and Schribner, 1965; Myers and Roberts, 1959; Myers and associates, 1968). Often they fail to even admit its presence until there is overt psychotic behavior present. Frequently, outside help is asked only when a person becomes a threat and a danger to himself or others. And, just as frequently, the first "help" they receive is from the police who are called in for protection from the mentally ill person. Too often the family tries to keep the disturbed member at home until it is too late and he becomes unmanageable.

There are many cultural reasons for this. Many still consider mental illness to be inherited and passed on from generation to generation. To admit it is "in the family" could destroy any pending marriages, business associations, and, most certainly, the family status in the community.

Realistically there is good reason for the lower classes to fear it. Hollingshead and Redlich's study (1958) shows that Class V individuals had the greatest percentage who were in state hospitals and receiving custodial care.

Class V individuals saw mental illness as craziness, not as being sick. For this they saw only institutionalization as the answer. Fearing this end, they avoided seeking any help, even when it was obviously needed.

Other factors have been recognized as pertinent, basic needs of the lower sociocultural groups that must be met in treatment programs (Bloch, 1968; Hartog, 1967; McMahon, 1964; Riessman and Schribner, 1965; Yamamoto and Goin, 1965). Generally, they are oriented to the here and now; they cannot afford to wait for tomorrow and later. Too often theirs is a day-by-day existence. They have no reason to save up for a rainy day because for them it may rain every day.

Long-term therapy is not for them if for no other reason than its cost. If a day laborer has to choose between keeping a clinic appointment and getting a few hours' work, he will have to have concrete proof that he will get help if he keeps the appointment and will expect immediate feelings of relief for his symptoms.

The lower sociocultural families have had long experience with help from outsiders, and the past history of social intervention from outsiders has not done much to build their trust. Many have learned to mistrust the well-intentioned social welfare agencies that saw fit to move the aged or infirm away from their homes and into institutions "for their own good." They are familiar with situations in which children have been taken from "unfit" parents and placed in foster homes or similar child-care agencies. Too often their families have been measured against middle-class norms and found lacking in stability. Ineffective outside action has led only to further instability. How can they be expected to trust the mental health profession? Historically it has taken either adverse actions against them or neglected them completely.

Even more concretely, until they have active proof that conversation or "talking treatment" will help them, their basic needs for survival will outweigh any appeals from them for their emotional needs. Not knowing what to expect or value from psychiatry, they cannot be expected to immediately feed back their needs.

The following case study illustrates how a therapist worked effectively in crisis intervention with a married couple whose sociocultural background was different from her own.

Case study

Tony and Marta, a young married couple with four small children, came to a crisis intervention center and requested help. They had originally gone to their parish priest for advice, and he had recommended that they seek professional help at a nearby community center. Tony was an unskilled laborer who worked for an airline as a maintenance man. He had finished the eighth grade in school; Marta had finished nine years of school and had worked in a garment factory until right before the birth of their first child. They lived in a poor section of town in a house owned by Tony's mother. Their only recreation was watching television. Tony usually worked six or seven days a week.

Tony was very angry and suspicious at the beginning of the session, whereas Marta appeared frightened and was reluctant to talk. When asked by the therapist as to "why they had come to the center," Tony replied that he thought his wife was crazy; he then began to explain her "crazy" behavior. The afternoon before,

Marta had caught their oldest son (Joe, 9 years old) playing with matches behind the house. She flew into a rage, pulled him into the house, and burned his arm by holding it over the flame of the kitchen stove. Tony's mother had walked in while Joe was screaming. The grandmother learned what had happened, and she had grabbed Marta and forced her arm over the flame so she "could see how it felt." When the therapist asked Marta if this were "true," she nodded her head and began to cry. The therapist asked if she could see her arm. Together they removed the bandage; it was a rather large, second-degree burn. Marta said she had put a patented burn medicine on it and a dressing. The therapist told Marta that she would like the doctor to see her arm to give her an antibiotic prescription and some medicine to help her control herself. A medical consultation was arranged and while Marta saw the physician, the therapist met with Tony.

(Therapist's note: This maneuver served two purposes: first, it showed Marta and Tony that she wanted to provide immediate help; and, second, by her non-judgmental attitude and acceptance of their behavior, she established a basis for rapport.)

When Tony was alone with the therapist, he dropped his defensive attitude and showed his true concern for Marta's irrational behavior. When questioned about Marta's usual manner of coping with problems, he stated that he really did not know—usually she just "blew up" at him, and since it did not bother him, he ignored it. He stated that he loved his wife and children and he believed that she loved him and the children, too. When asked what he and Marta usually did together and with the children for pleasure, he said, "Are you kidding? I work six or seven days a week . . . hard! I come home and I'm tired; I have a few beers, eat, and usually fall asleep in front of T.V." When asked what Marta usually did, he stated that she "took care of the house and kids."

When Marta returned from the medical consultation, the therapist repeated what Tony had told her. Marta said, "That's true . . . that's *all* I do: take care of his mother's crummy house and the kids!" Tony jumped on this immediately and said, "You have never gotten along with my mother . . . you hate her!" Marta said that she did not hate her . . . she just did not like her "always butting into our business and you always taking her side against me and the kids! I've told you I don't like living in her house, where she can walk in and out anytime she wants to; I want a place I can call my own. We pay her rent; we can pay rent someplace else . . . and get a better house too!"

Tony said, "You never told me you didn't want to live in Mother's house." Marta said, "I have . . . but you never listen!"

When asked about the possibility of moving, since Marta was unhappy with the living arrangements, Tony said his mother would "not understand," but "Marta and the kids mean more to me than anything."

The therapist thought at this time she could refocus on the problem that had brought them into the center. She asked Marta about burning Joe's arm. Marta said, "I was tired and upset; all I ever hear are the kids yelling and Tony's mother butting in and telling me everything I'm doing wrong . . . with the kids and the house; and Tony never tries to help or even listen to me. I just felt like I was cracking up!"

Tony was asked if there were any way he could help Marta. It was explained that it can be very exhausting taking care of four small children every day without a few hours "off." The therapist went on to tell Tony that his work kept him in contact with people all day, whereas Marta had no contact with anyone except his mother (who was an added irritant) and the children. Marta said that if only she could look forward to talking with him when she was upset, or even if she could go over to a friend's house for a few hours once or twice a week, "anything to get away for a few hours!" she knew she would be all right.

Tony very reluctantly said that he would put the kids to bed one night for her so she could go to a friend's house. The therapist said that it sounded like a wonderful idea and that what would really be good for them both would be if they could get out for a few hours together to talks things over. Their reaction was a cautious silence.

When Tony and Marta came for their next session, it was very obvious that they had had a good week. They were talking together quite animatedly when the therapist came into the waiting room to get them for their appointment. She remarked how well they looked, and how happy. Marta started talking about their week: Tony had put the kids to bed one night, as he had said he would, and she had gone to a friend's house to visit. She said it was really great to be out for a few hours. When Tony was asked how he had managed with the children, he looked embarrassed and said, "It was a mess! I don't know how she ever manages them all; no wonder she gets so tired!" It seemed that Tony could not get the children to go to sleep—or even stay in bed—without Marta there to control them. What he finally did was bring them all into the living room to watch television, and when they fell asleep, he carried them one by one to bed. The highlight of the week came when Tony told his mother not to come to the house and bother Marta. He had said that if she did, he and Marta would find another house and move. This made Marta feel so much better that she backed down a bit and told her mother-in-law that she could visit them but that she ought to call in advance to say that she was coming. The therapist told them how well they were doing in working toward solving their problem but cautioned them that there would be good weeks and bad weeks and if they began to talk *with* each other when problems arose rather than *at* each other, they could work out solutions more easily.

At the next session Marta had apparently stabilized, and Tony and she were relaxed and comfortable with each other and the therapist. Tony began by saying that they both really felt that they were capable of handling their problems now and did not want to return for more visits. He said that he could really understand Marta's feelings of being "hemmed in" and "trapped" when she was with the children constantly, all day and every day. He said a friend at work had invited them over for dinner the Saturday before, and instead of refusing as he usually did he had accepted. He asked his mother to stay with the children, and he and Marta went to dinner. He said that as he watched Marta laughing and talking, he realized how much he had missed their being together, alone, "like before we were married. I watched her and realized how pretty and young she really is and how much I love her. I'm going to do everything I can to help her with the kids . . . I know we can make it now!" The therapist agreed and wished them luck and told them that if they needed help again to feel free to return to the center.

Summary of case study

The therapist in this situation, even though from a middle-class background, was aware of the sociocultural background of her patients, and this knowledge was invaluable in the approach. Her attitude was nonjudgmental, concentrated on getting some immediate "help" (the medical consultation), and focused on assisting them with their problem. No attempt was made at characterological or insightful changes in their behavior, but she worked on the "here and now" and was very directive. Although she offered suggestions, no attempt was made at major changes in behavior. The terminology was kept at a concrete level, so she was able to talk with them in language they could understand. She attempted to give them the feeling that she was there to help them and that she would be there in the future if necessary.

CONCLUSIONS

It is our contention that crisis intervention is one logical treatment modality for those in the lower sociocultural classes. It can fulfill their needs for immediate problem solving, it is direct and short term, and the therapist's role in it is an active one. No attempt is made to produce drastic behavioral changes. Its object is to reduce the symptoms of disequilibrium and to restore the individual to a precrisis level of functioning, with improved abilities to solve problems and more effective coping skills.

Community mental health centers, rather than large, isolated institutions, are where the "people" are. If therapists are to work successfully with the poor or disadvantaged, they should understand and accept the possibility that those who seek their help may have different attitudes and values. It should be the therapists' commitment to learn how to communicate with and meet the needs of those who seek help. The burden should not be placed upon them to change their life style and patterns of living in order to get the help they are seeking.

REFERENCES

Albronda, H. F., Dean, R. L., and Stark-weather, J. A.: Social class and psychotherapy, Arch. Gen. Psychiatry **10**:276-283, 1964.

Benedict, Ruth: Anthropology and the abnormal, J. Gen. Psychol. **10**:59-82, 1934.

Bloch, H. Spencer: An open-ended crisis-oriented group for the poor who are sick, Arch. Gen. Psychiatry **18**:178-185, Feb. 1968.

Brill, N. Q., and Storrow, H. A.: Social class and psychiatric treatment, Arch. Gen. Psychiatry **3**:340-344, 1960.

Haas, Kurt: The middle-class professional

and the lower-class patient, Ment. Hyg. **47:**408-410, 1963.

Hartog, Joseph: The mental health problems of poverty's youth, Ment. Hyg. **51:**85-90, Jan. 1967.

Heine, R. W., and Trossman, J.: Initial expectations of the doctor-patient interaction as a factor in continuance in psychotherapy, Psychiatry **23:**275-278, Aug. 1960.

Hollingshead, A. B., and Redlich, F. C.: Social class and mental illness, New York, 1958, John Wiley & Sons, Inc.

Jacobson, Gerald F.: Crisis theory and treatment strategy; some sociocultural and psychodynamic considerations, J. Nerv. Ment. Dis. **141:**209-217, Aug. 1965.

McMahon, J. T.: The working class psychiatric patient; a clinical view. In Riessman, F., and others, editors: Mental health of the poor, New York, 1964, The Free Press, Division of The Macmillan Co.

Myers, Jerome K., Bean, Leo L., and Pepper, Max P.: A decade later; a follow-up of social class and mental illness, New York, 1968, John Wiley & Sons, Inc.

Myers, Jerome K., and Roberts, Bertram H.: Family and class dynamics in mental illness, New York, 1959, John Wiley & Sons, Inc.

Opler, Marvin K.: Culture, psychiatry and human values, Springfield, Ill., 1956, Charles C Thomas, Publisher.

Redlich, F. C.: The concept of normality, Am. J. Psychother. **6:**551-576, 1952. Republished in Bergen, B. J., and Thomas, C. S., editors: Issues and problems in social psychiatry, Springfield, Ill., 1966, Charles C Thomas, Publisher, pp. 85-105.

Riessman, F., and Miller, S. M.: Social change versus the psychiatric world view, Am. J. Orthopsychiatry **34:** 29-38, Jan. 1964.

Riessman, F., and Scribner, S.: The underutilization of mental health services by workers and low income groups; causes and cures, Am. J. Psychiatry **121:**798-801, Feb. 1965.

Seward, Georgene: Psychotherapy and culture conflict, New York, 1956, The Ronald Press Co.

Tershakovek, Andrew: An observation concerning changing attitudes toward mental illness, Am. J. Psychiatry **121:**353-357, Oct. 1964.

Yamamoto, J., and Goin, M. L.: On the treatment of the poor, Am. J. Psychiatry **122:**267-271, Sept. 1965.

ADDITIONAL READINGS

Adams, Paul L., and McDonald, F.: Clinical cooling out of poor people, Am. J. Orthopsychiatry **38:**457-463, April 1968.

Chilman, Catherine S.: Growing up poor, Washington, D. C., 1969, U. S. Department of Health, Education, and Welfare.

Cobb, Charles W.: Community health services and the lower socioeconomic classes; a summary of research literature on outpatient treatment (1963-1969), Am. J. Orthopsychiatry **42:**404-414, April 1972.

Lilienfeld, D.: Mental health information and moral values of lower-class psychiatric clinic patients, J. Soc. Psychiatry **15:**264-278, 1969.

5 Problem-solving approach to crisis intervention

According to Caplan,[1] man is constantly faced with a need to solve problems in order to maintain equilibrium. When he is confronted with an imbalance between the difficulty (as he perceives it) of a problem and his available repertoire of coping skills, a crisis may be precipitated. If alternatives cannot be found or if solving the problem requires more time and energy than is usual, disequilibrium occurs. Tension rises and discomfort is felt, with associated feelings of anxety, fear, guilt, shame, and helplessness.

One purpose of the crisis approach is to provide the consultation services of a therapist skilled in problem-solving techniques. This does not mean that the therapist will have an answer to every problem. However, he will be expected to have a ready and knowledgeable competency in problem solving, guiding and supporting his client toward crisis resolution. The therapeutic goal for the individual seeking help is the establishment of a level of emotional equilibrium equal to or better than his precrisis level.

Problem solving requires that a logical sequence of reasoning be applied to a situation in which an answer is required for a question and in which there is no immediate source of reliable information.[2] This process may take place either consciously or unconsciously. Usually the need to find an answer or solution is felt more strongly where such a resolution is most difficult

The problem-solving process follows a structured, logical order of steps, each depending upon the one preceding. In the routine decision making required in daily living, this process is rarely necessary. Most people are unaware that they may follow a defined, logical sequence of reasoning in making decisions, often only remarking that some solutions seem to have been reached more easily than others.

---

[1]Caplan, Gerald: Principles of preventive psychiatry, New York, 1964, Basic Books, Inc., Publishers, p. 38.
[2]Black, Max: Critical thinking; an introduction to logic and scientific method, Englewood Cliffs, N. J., 1946, Prentice-Hall, Inc., pp. 247-248.

Finding out the time or deciding which shoe to put on first rarely calls for long, involved reasoning, and more often than not the question arises and the answer is found without any conscious effort.

FACTORS AFFECTING THE PROBLEM-SOLVING PROCESS

Depending upon the past experience related to the immediate problem, some people will be more adept at finding solutions than others. Both internal and external factors affect the process at any given time, although initially there may be only a temporary lack of concrete information. For example, when a driver finds himself lost because of a missing road sign, how much finding the right directions means to him in terms of his physical, psychological, and social well-being could affect the ease with which he finds an answer to the problem. Anxiety will increase in proportion to the value he places upon finding a solution. If he is only out driving for pleasure, for example, he may feel casually concerned; but if he is under stress to be somewhere on time, his anxiety may increase according to the importance of his arrival to his immediate goals.

When anxiety is kept within tolerable limits, it can be an effective stimulant to action. It is a normal response to an unknown danger, experienced as discomfort, and helps the individual to mobilize his resources in meeting the problem. But as anxiety increases, there is a narrowing of perceptual awareness, and all perceptions are focused on the difficulty. When problem-solving skills are available, the individual is able to use this narrowing of perceptions to concentrate on the problem at hand.

If a solution is not found, anxiety may become more severe. Feelings of discomfort become intensified, and perceptions are narrowed to a crippling degree. The ability to understand what is happening and to make use of past experiences gives way to concentration on the discomfort itself. The individual becomes unable to recognize his own feelings, the problem, the facts, the evidence, and the situation in which he finds himself.[3]

Although problem solving involves a logical sequence of reasoning, it is not *always* a series of well-defined steps. According to Myer and Heidgerken (1962), it usually begins with a feeling that something has to be done. The problem area is generalized rather than made specific and well defined. Next, there is a search of the memory in an attempt to come up with ideas or solutions from similar problems in the past. March and Simon (1963) refer to this as "reproductive problem-solving," and its value is greatly dependent upon past successes in finding solutions.

When no similar past experiences are available, the individual may next turn to "productive problem solving." Here he is faced with the need to construct new ideas from more or less raw data. He will have to go to sources other than himself to get his facts. For example, the driver looking for the road sign may find someone

---

[3]Peplau, Hildegarde E.: Interpersonal relations in nursing, New York, 1952, G. P. Putnam's Sons, pp. 127-128.

nearby who can give him the needed new data; directions to the right road. If there is no one nearby, he will have to find some other source of information. He may resort to trial and error and with luck and patience find the way himself. Finding a solution in this way may meet a present need, but the information gained may not always be applicable to solving a similar problem in the future.

PROBLEM SOLVING IN CRISIS INTERVENTION

John Dewey (1910) proposed the classical steps or stages represented in different episodes of problem solving: (1) a difficulty is felt, (2) the difficulty is located and defined, (3) possible solutions are suggested, (4) consequences are considered, and (5) a solution is accepted. With minor modifications, these steps in problem solving have been persistent over the years. Johnson (1955) simplified problem solving by reducing the number of steps to three: preparation, production, and judgment.

In 1962 Merrifield and associates conducted extensive research on the role of intellectual factors in problem solving. They advocated return to a five-stage model, with preparation, analysis, production, verification, and reapplication. The fifth term was included in recognition of the fact that the problem solver often returns to earlier stages in a kind of revolving fashion.

According to Guilford (1967), the general problem-solving model involves the following process. (1) *input* (from environment and soma), (2) *filtering* (attention aroused and directed), (3) *cognition* (problem sensed and structured), (4) *production* (answers generated), (5) *cognition* (new information obtained), (6) *production* (new answers generated), (7) *evaluation* (input and cognition tested, answers tested; new tests of problem structure, new answers tested).

Assessment of the individual and his problem

When professional help is sought because a person is in crisis, the therapist must use logic and background knowledge to define the problem and plan intervention. The model for problem solving in the crisis approach will be readily familiar to nurses who have become skilled in making nursing judgments. It will be particularly familiar to mental health nurses.

The crisis approach to problem solving involves[4] an assessment of the individual and his problem, planning of therapeutic intervention, intervention, and resolution of the crisis and anticipatory planning.

Assessment begins when the individual requesting help is seen by a therapist. The first therapy session is directed toward finding out what the crisis-precipitating event was and what factors are affecting his ability to solve problems.

It is important that both therapist and patient be able to define a situation clearly before taking any action to change it. Questions are asked such as "What

---

[4]Morley, Wilbur E., Messick, Janice M., and Aguilera, Donna C.: Crisis; paradigms of intervention, J. Psychiatr. Nurs. **5:**538-540, Nov.-Dec. 1967.

do I need to know?" and "What must be done?" The more specifically the problem can be defined the more likely it is that the "correct" answer will be sought.

Clues are investigated to point out and explore the problem or what is happening. The therapist asks questions and uses observational skills to obtain factual knowledge about the problem area. It is important to know what has happened within the immediate situation. How the individual has coped in past situations may affect his present behavior. Observations are made to determine his level of anxiety, expressive movements, emotional tone, verbal responses, and attitudinal changes.

It is important to remember that the therapist's task is that of focusing on the immediate problem. There is not enough time and *no need* to go into the patient's past history in depth.

One of the therapist's first questions usually is, "Why did you come for help today?" It is important to be emphatic about using the word *today*. Sometimes the individual will try to *avoid* stating why he came by saying: "I've been planning to come for some time." The usual reply is, "Yes, but what happened that made you come in *today*?" Other questions to ask are, "What hapepned in your life that is *different? When* did it happen?"

In crisis the precipitating event usually has occurred within ten to fourteen days before the individual seeks help. Frequently it is something that happened the day before or the night before. It could be almost anything: threat of divorce, discovery of extramarital relations, finding out their son or daughter is on drugs, loss of boyfriend or girlfriend, loss of job or status, an unwanted pregnancy, and so forth.

The next area on which to focus is the individual's perception of the event: What does it mean to him? How does he see its effect on his future? Does he see the event realistically, or does he distort its meaning?

The patient is then questioned about available situational supports: What person in the environment can the therapist find to support the person? With whom does he live? Who is his best friend? Whom does he trust? Is there a member of the family to whom he feels particularly close? Crisis intervention is sharply time limited, and the more people involved in helping the person the better. Also, when therapy is terminated, if others are involved and familiar with the problem they can continue to give support.

The next area of focus is to ascertain what the person usually does when he has a problem he cannot solve: What are his coping skills? He is asked the following: Has anything like this ever happened to him before? How does he usually abate tension, anxiety, or depression? Has he tried the same method this time? If not, why not, if it usually works for him? If his usual method was tried and it did not work, the therapist asks, *why*. What does he feel would reduce his symptoms of stress? Something is usually thought of; coping skills are so very individual. Methods of coping with anxiety that have not been used in years may be remembered. One man recalled that he used to "work off tensions" by playing the piano for a few hours, and it was suggested that he try this method again. Since he did not have a piano, he rented one; by the next session his anxiety had reduced enough to enable him to begin problem solving.

One of the most important parts of the assessment is to find out whether the individual is suicidal or homicidal. The questions must be very *direct* and *specific:* Is he planning to kill himself or someone else? How? When? The therapist must find out and assess the seriousness of the threat: Is he merely thinking about it or does he have a method selected? Is it a lethal method—a loaded gun? Is a tall building or bridge picked out? Can he tell you when he plans to do it—for example, after the children are asleep?

If the threat does not seem too imminent, the individual is accepted for crisis therapy. If the intent is carefully planned and details are specific, hospitalization and psychiatric evaluation are arranged in order to protect him or others in the community.

Planning of therapeutic intervention

After identifying the precipitating event and the factors that are influencing the individual's state of disequilibrium, the therapist plans the method of intervention. Determination must be made as to how much the crisis has disrupted the individual's life. Is he able to work? Go to school? Keep house? Care for his family? Are these activities being affected? This is the first area to examine for the degree of disruption. How is his state of disequilibrium affecting others in his life? How does his wife (or husband, boyfriend, girlfriend, roommate, or family) feel about this problem? What do they think he should do? Are they upset?

This is basically a search process in which data are collected. It requires the use of cognitive abilities and recollection of past events for information relative to the present situation. The last phase of this step is essentially a thinking process in which alternatives are considered and evaluated against past experience and knowledge as well as in the context of the present situation.

Tentative solutions are advanced as to *why* the problem exists. This requires familiarity with theoretical knowledge and the anticipation of more than one answer. In the study of behavior it is important to seek causal relationships. Clues observed in the environmental conditions are examined and related to theories of psychosocial behavior to suggest reasons for the individual's disturbed equilibrium.

Intervention

In the third step intervention is initiated. Action is taken with the expectation that if _____ is taken, the _____ will occur.
          (planned action)   (expected result)

After the necessary information is collected, the problem-solving process is continued to initiate intervention. The therapist defines the problem from the information that has been given and reflects it back to the individual. This clarifies the problem and encourages focusing on the immediate situation. The therapist then explores possible alternate solutions to the problem to reduce the symptoms produced by the crisis. At this time, specific directions may be given as to what should be tried as tentative solutions. This enables the individual to leave the first session with some positive guidelines for going out and testing alternate solutions. At the next session the individual and therapist evaluate the results, and if none of these solutions has been effective, they work toward finding others.

The therapist may validate observations and tentative conclusions by reviewing the case with another therapist when deeming that it may be helpful or necessary. Briefly, the therapist identifies the crisis-precipitating event, symptoms that the crisis has produced in the individual, the degree of disruption evident in the individual's life, and the plan for intervention. Planned intervention may include one technique or a combination of several techniques. It may be helping the individual to gain an intellectual understanding of the crisis or helping him to explore and ventilate his feelings. Other techniques may be helping the individual to find new and more effective coping mechanisms or utilizing other people as situational supports. Finally, a plan would be presented for helping the person to establish realistic goals for the future.

Anticipatory planning

Evaluation is made to determine whether or not the planned action has produced the expected results. Appraisal must be objective and impartial in order to be valid. Has the individual returned to his usual or higher level of equilibrium in his functioning? The problem-solving process is continued as the therapist and the individual work toward resolution of the crisis.

PARADIGM OF INTERVENTION

According to Caplan,[5] there are four developmental phases in a crisis:

1. There is an initial rise in tension as habitual problem-solving techniques are tried.

2. There is a lack of success in coping as the stimulus continues and more discomfort is felt.

3. A further increase in tension acts as a powerful internal stimulus and mobilizes internal and external resources. In this stage emergency problem-solving mechanisms are tried. The problem may be redefined or there may be resignation and the giving up of certain aspects of the goal as unattainable.

4. If the problem continues and can neither be solved nor avoided, tension increases and a major disorganization occurs.

Whenever a stressful event occurs, there are certain recognized balancing factors that can effect a return to equilibrium; these are perception of the event, available situational supports, and coping mechanisms as shown in Fig. 1. The upper portion of the paradigm illustrates the "normal" initial reaction of an individual to a stressful event.

A stressful event is seldom so clearly defined that its source can be determined immediately. Internalized changes occur at the same time as the externally provoked stress, and as a result, some events may cause a strong emotional response

---

[5]Caplan: Principles of preventive psychiatry, pp. 40-41.

Human organism

Stressful event ⟶ State of equilibrium ⟵ Stressful event

State of disequilibrium

Felt need to
restore equilibrium

A
Balancing factors present

B
One or more balancing factors absent

* Realistic perception of
the event

Distorted perception
of the event

plus

and/or

* Adequate
situational support

No adequate
situational support

plus

and/or

* Adequate
coping mechanisms

No
coping mechanisms

result in

result in

Resolution
of the problem

Problem
unresolved

Equilibrium
regained

Disequilibrium
continues

No crisis

Crisis

*Balancing factors.

Fig. 1. Paradigm: effect of balancing factors in a stressful event.

Fig. 2. Paradigm applied to case studies.

in one person, yet leave another apparently unaffected. Much is determined by the presence or absence of factors that can effect a return to equilibrium.

In column *A* of Fig. 1 the balancing factors are operating and crisis is avoided. However, in column *B* the absence of one or more of these balancing factors may block resolution of the problem, thus increasing disequilibrium and precipitating crisis.

Fig. 2 demonstrates the use of the paradigm for presentation of subsequent case studies. Its purpose is to serve as a guideline to focus the reader on the problem areas. An example of its applicability is presented in the cases of two people affected by the same stressful event. One resolved the problem and avoided crisis; the other did not.

BALANCING FACTORS AFFECTING EQUILIBRIUM

Between the perceived effects of a stressful situation and the resolution of the problem are three recognized balancing factors that may determine the state of equilibrium. Strengths or weaknesses in any one of these factors can be directly related to the onset of crisis or to its resolution. These are perception of the event, available situational supports, and coping mechanisms.

Why do some people go into crisis when others do not? In Fig. 2 this is illustrated by the cases of two students, Sue and Mary. Both fail a final examination. Sue is upset but does not go into crisis. Mary *does* go into crisis. Why does Sue react one way and Mary differently to the same stressful event? What "things" in their present lives make the difference?

Perception of the event

If the event is perceived realistically, there will be recognition of the relationship between the event and feelings of stress. Problem solving can be appropriately oriented toward reduction of tension, and successful solution of the stressful situation will be more probable.

If the perception of the event is distorted, there may be no recognition of a relationship between the event and feelings of stress. Thus attempts to solve the problem will be ineffective, and tension will not be reduced.

In other words, what does the event mean to the individual? How is it going to affect his future? Can he look at it realistically, or does he distort its meaning? For example, Sue sees failing the examination as the result of not studying enough or of concentrating on the wrong material and decides it will not happen again. Mary, on the other hand, thinks that failing the examination makes *her* a failure; she feels threatened and believes she will never graduate from college.

Situational supports

By nature, man is social and dependent upon others in his environment to supply him with reflected appraisals of his own intrinsic and extrinsic values. In establishing his life patterns, certain appraisals are more significant to him than others because they tend to reinforce the perception he has of himself. Dependency relationships may be more readily established with those whose appraisals tend to support the individual against feelings of insecurity and who reinforce feelings of ego integrity.

Loss, threatened loss, or feelings of inadequacy in a supportive relationship may leave the individual in a vulnerable position, so that when confronted with a stressful situation, the lack of situational support may lead to a state of disequilibrium and possible crisis.

Situational supports mean those persons who are available in the environment who can be depended upon to help solve the problem.

Sue talked to her roommate about her feelings over failing the exam; she even cried on her shoulder. She also called home for reassurance from her family. In effect, *someone* had been found for support during this stressful event.

Mary did not feel close enough to her roommate to talk about the problem. She had no close friends whom she trusted. Fearing their reaction, she did not call home to tell her family about failing. Mary did not have *anyone* to turn to for help; she felt overwhelmed and alone.

Coping mechanisms

Through the process of daily living the individual learns to use many methods to cope with anxiety and reduce tension. Life styles are developed around patterns of response, which in turn are established to cope with stressful situations. These life styles are highly individual and quite necessary to protect and maintain equilibrium.

Tension-reducing mechanisms can be overt or covert and can be consciously or unconsciously activated. They have been generally classified into such behavioral responses as aggression, regression, withdrawal, and repression. The selection of a response is based upon tension-reducing actions that successfully relieved anxiety and reduced tension in similar situations in the past. Through repetition it may pass from conscious awareness during its learning phase to a habitual level of reaction as a learned behavior. In many instances the individual may not be aware of *how,* let alone *why,* he reacts to stress in given situations. Except for vague feelings of discomfort, the rise and consequent reduction in tension may pass almost unnoticed. When a novel stress-producing event arises and learned coping mechanisms are ineffectual, discomfort is felt on a conscious level. The need to "do something" becomes the focus of activity, narrowing perception of all other life activities.

Available coping mechanisms are what people *usually* do when they have a problem. They may sit down and try to think it out or talk it out with a friend. Some cry it out or try to get rid of their feelings of anger and hostility by swearing, kicking a chair, or slamming doors. Others may get into verbal battles with friends. Some may react by temporarily withdrawing from the situation in order to reassess the problem. These are just a few of the many coping methods people use to relieve their tension and anxiety when faced with a problem. Each of these has been used at some time in the developmental past of the individual, found effective to maintain emotional stability, and become part of his life style in meeting and dealing with the stresses of daily living.

Sue used her roommate to talk it out; this reduced her tension and anxiety. She was able to solve the problem and decided that for the next exam she would study more, over a longer period of time. Her tension and anxiety were reduced, equilibrium was restored, and she did not have a crisis.

Mary withdrew. She had no coping skills to use, and her tension and anxiety increased. Unable to solve the problem and unable to function, she went into crisis.

REFERENCES

Dewey, John: How we think, Boston, 1910, Heath Co.

Guilford, J. P.: The nature of human intelligence, New York, 1967, McGraw-Hill Book Co.

Johnson, D. M.: The psychology of thought and judgment, New York, 1955, Harper & Row, Publishers.

March, James G., and Simon, Herbert A.: Organizations, New York, 1963, John Wiley & Sons, Inc.

Merrifield, P. R., Guilford, J. P., Christensen, P. R., and Frick, J. W.: The role of intellectual factors in problem-solving, Psychol. Monogr. 76(10), 1962.

Myer, Burton, and Heidgerken, Loretta E.: Introduction to research in nursing, Philadelphia, 1962, J. B. Lippincott Co.

6 Situational crises

Whenever stressful events occur in a person's life situation that threaten his sense of biological, psychological, or social integrity, there is some degree of disequilibrium resulting and the concurrent possibility of a crisis. Several determining factors affect the positive balance of equilibrium, and the absence of one or more could make a state of crisis more imminent.

According to Rapoport,[1] when an instinctual need or a sense of integrity is threatened, the ego usually responds characteristically with anxiety; when loss or deprivation occur, the response is usually depression. On the other hand, if the threat or loss is viewed as a challenge, there is more likely to be a mobilization of energy toward purposeful problem-solving activities.

That which may create only a feeling of mild concern in one person may create a high level of anxiety and tension in another. Recognized factors influencing a return to a balance of equilibrium are the perception of the event, available coping mechanisms, and available situational supports. Crises may be avoided if these factors are operating at the time the stressful event(s) is intruding into the individual's life style.

Studies have been made of behavior patterns that might be anticipated in response to common stressful situations. These have provided valuable clues to anticipatory planning for prevention as well as intervention in crisis situations. Some of these are combat neurosis (Glass, 1957), relocation through urban renewal (Brown and associates, 1965), rehabilitation of families after tornado disasters (Moore, 1958), hospitalized children and adolescents (Vernick, 1963), unwed mothers (Bernstein, 1960), and separation anxiety of hospitalized children (Bowlby, 1960). These studies suggest that there are certain patterned phases of reactions to unique stressful situations through which select groups of people can be expected to pass before equilibrium is restored. Preventive techniques of community psy-

---

[1]Rapoport, Lydia: The state of crisis; some theoretical considerations, Social Service Rev. **36:**211-217, 1962.

chiatry focus on anticipatory intervention; this is to prevent crises that could result from maladaptive responses as individuals attempt to return to equilibrium.

In this chapter, stressful events that could precipitate a crisis have been selected on the premise that each could affect some member of a family, regardless of its socioeconomic or sociocultural status. The case studies selected are not to be considered all-inclusive of the many situational crises with which a therapist may come in contact.

It is also important to recognize that the theoretical material preceding each case study is presented as an overview, relevant to the crisis situation. Those therapists already trained in crisis intervention will recognize the need for much greater depth of theoretical knowledge than is presented in this chapter. The intent is only to provide guidelines; further study of problem areas is suggested for more comprehensive knowledge.

In order to clarify the steps in crisis intervention, much extraneous case study material has been eliminated. In crisis a person may be confronted with *many* stressful events occurring simultaneously. He may have no conscious awareness of *what* occurred, let alone which event requires priority in problem solving. The studies may appear oversimplified to anyone who has struggled through the phases of defining the problem and planning appropriate intervention.

The paradigm is a means we devised to keep the reader focused on the problem area and on the balancing factors that influence the presence or absence of crisis. We doubt if it could be successfully used as a form that could be quickly completed after the initial assessment interview; rarely are stressful events so easily defined. It is the very nature of a crisis that interrelated internal and external stresses compound the problem area and distort the causes of objective and subjective symptoms.

One responsibility essential in assuming the role of a therapist in this method of intervention is recognition of the need for knowledge of the generic development of crises.

PREMATURITY
Theoretical concepts

The birth of a premature baby is a stressful situation for any family. Even when anticipated, there is a sense of emergency both at home and in the hospital when labor begins. In the hospital, both staff and parents feel anxiety for the potential welfare of the newborn infant.

Researchers have identified the following four phases or tasks the mother must work through if she is to come out of the experience in a healthy way.[2,3]

---

[2]Mason, E. A.: Method of predicting crisis outcome for mothers of premature babies, Public Health Rep. **78:**1031-1035, Dec. 1963.
[3]Kaplan, D. M., and Mason, E. A.: Maternal reactions to premature birth viewed as an acute emotional disorder. In Pard, H. J., editor: Crisis intervention, New York, 1965, Family Service Association of America, pp. 118-128.

1. She must realize that she may lose the baby. This anticipatory grief involves a gradual withdrawal from the relationship already established with the child during the pregnancy.

2. She must acknowledge failure in her maternal function to deliver a full-term baby.

3. After separation from the infant due to its prolonged hospital stay she must resume her relationship with it in preparation for the infant's homecoming.

4. She must prepare herself for the job of caring for the baby through an understanding of its special needs and growth patterns.

After delivery the infant is hurriedly taken to the premature nursery. The parents have barely had a glimpse of their new son or daughter and certainly have had no opportunity to reassure themselves about its condition. The infant is isolated from all except the medical personnel during its hospital stay, and the parents, denied physical contact with the child, cannot allay their anxieties. There is a realistic danger that the baby will not live or that it will not be normal. Often doctors and nurses talk about the baby in guarded terms, not wanting to give false reassurance, so that the feeling of anxiety may last for days or weeks.

The way in which the family reacts to this period of stress is crucial in determining whether or not a crisis will develop. These studies of families who have experienced the stress of a premature birth show that some have managed very well; the mother was not apprehensive about caring for the baby, despite the special attention it required. In these families the relationship between husband and wife was found to be good; they seemingly had adjusted to the new member of the family, and their relationship was not threatened by the increased responsibility.

Other families studied appeared to be in a state of crisis, although the premature infant was out of danger. In those cases the relationship between the husband and wife was determined to be unstable. The baby was cared for by an overly apprehensive mother who often seemed unconcerned about important things such as his weight gain, whether or not he was eating adequately, and his immediate prognosis.

It has been hypothesized that women who were most disturbed during the period when there was real danger to the baby dealt with this stress more effectively.[4] Women who showed symptoms of a crisis were those who seemingly denied the existence of any danger. They did not question the information given them nor the reassurances of the treating personnel. In fact, they seemed to encourage a conspiracy of silence, avoiding any confrontation with feelings of fear, guilt, and anxiety.

Many emotions develop in parents when a new baby arrives, even when the

---

[4]Caplan, Gerald: Principles of preventive psychiatry, New York, 1964, Basic Books, Inc., Publishers, p. 290.

child is full term. The mother is called upon to meet additional demands upon her time and may feel hostility toward the new baby. Usually, however, the strong feeling of mother love ensures repression of any resentment she may feel and the guilt it inspires. The usual activities of the father are not as directly interrupted, so that his resentment is usually less than that of the mother and is more often aroused by jealousy of the attention that the mother gives to the baby.

The following case study concerns a young mother of a premature baby. Clues from the initial assessment interview indicated that she was acknowledging herself to be a failure for not delivering a full-term baby. Intervention focused on relieving the immediate causes of her anxiety and depression and assisting her to adapt to subsequent phases in the characteristic responses to a premature birth.

Case study: Prematurity
Assessment of the individual and his problem

Laura and Peter G. were a young couple who had been married for three years. Peter, five years older than Laura, was the oldest of four children. Laura, a petite young woman, was an only child. They had a daughter 2 years old and a son 2 months of age who was born prematurely.

Peter's company had transferred him to another city when Laura was seven and one-half months pregnant; she went into labor the day after moving into their new home 100 miles from their home town, where both their families lived. She delivered their son in a private hospital with excellent facilities but under the care of an obstetrician previously unknown to her due to their recent move. She was upset by the strangeness of the hospital, by the new doctor, and by the precarious physical condition of the son she and Peter had been hoping for. Laura did not want to discuss her fears with Peter, because she knew he was also concerned about the baby, and she did not want to add to his worries. Laura did not feel free to discuss her fears with her doctor, because she did not know him, or with the nurses, because they "always seemed so busy." She also thought that since she had had a baby before, she should know the answers to all the questions she had in mind.

After she and Peter brought their son home from the hospital, Laura had episodes of crying and was experiencing symptoms of anxiety, including insomnia. She felt physically exhausted and increasingly fearful concerning her ability to care for her son. No matter what she did, the baby slept only for short periods and was more fretful when awake than their daughter had been. Because of the baby's small size, Peter was afraid to help with his care, so Laura was responsible for all his physical care.

Peter's mother arrived for a visit "to see how the new baby was doing." She had been critical of Laura's intention to move at the time of Peter's transfer, advising that Laura should wait until after the baby's birth. Laura had now begun to think that she should have followed that advice. Her mother-in-law and she often had talks about the rearing of children. Laura had begun to have confidence in her own mothering abilities as a result of her daughter's good health and average development, but now she was doubtful again because of her apparent inability to care for her new son.

Planning of therapeutic intervention

The event that precipitated the crisis was the visit of a mother-in-law who was critical of Laura's ability to care for her new baby. "I can't understand why the baby cries so much. You must be doing something wrong. My children always slept through the night by 2 months of age and took long naps during the day," were typical of her constant comments. Peter seemed reluctant to take sides against his mother, so Laura received little support from him in dealing with these criticisms. She was finally unable to cope with her feelings of inadequacy, which were intensified by her mother-in-law's visit, and as a result became extremely upset, cried uncontrollably, and was unable to care for the baby at all. Peter's employer commented to him that he seemed upset and asked if there was anything wrong at work. Peter told him that the problem was not his job but Laura's behavior since the birth of the baby. His employer recommended that they seek help at a nearby crisis intervention center.

The goal of intervention determined by the therapist at the crisis center was to assist both Laura and Peter in exploring their feelings regarding the premature birth of their son, their changed communication pattern, and the lack of support Peter was giving Laura.

Intervention

During the first few weeks, Laura was able to discuss her feelings of inadequacy in the mothering role and to tell Peter of her anxieties regarding their son, of her fears that he would be abnormal, and of her belief that the premature birth was her fault because she had insisted upon moving with Peter at the time of his transfer. Peter, in turn, could tell Laura of his feelings of guilt at not being able to help more during the move, and also of the blame he placed upon himself because the labor was premature. The therapist assisted them in seeing the reality of the situation. Although the move may have been a factor in the premature onset of labor, there could have been other causes.

Peter discussed his insecurities regarding the handling of such a small baby; Laura was then able to tell him that she felt the same way and she feared she might be doing something wrong with this baby. The therapist gave them information about the differences in the behavior of a normal child and the care required for a premature infant. She reassured Laura that she was doing well and that in time the baby would adjust to more regular hours. She also encouraged Peter to help his wife so that she could get more rest; in turn Laura helped Peter to gain confidence in holding and caring for their new son.

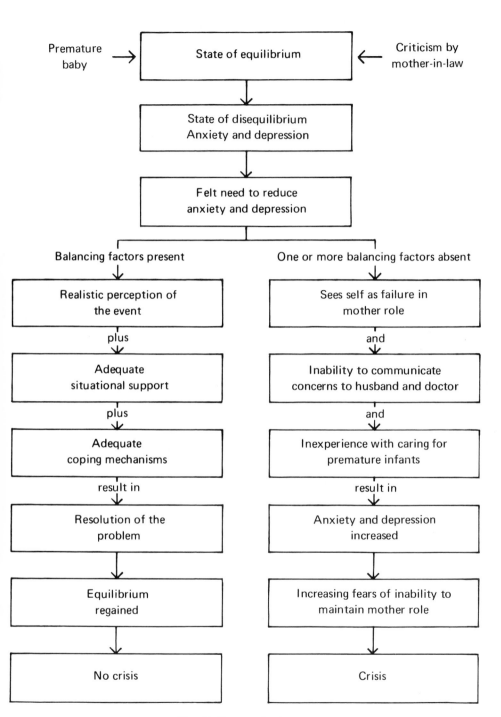

Fig. 3. Case study: Laura.

Anticipatory planning

As Peter became comfortable in caring for the baby, he was encouraged to share the responsibility of caring for him in the evenings. This enabled Laura to get more physical rest. Peter's emotional support helped her to relax, and she began to sleep better.

The therapist discussed their need to continue to improve communications between them. It was stressed that they must reestablish a pattern of social activities with each other. They were assured that their new son could survive for a few hours with a competent baby-sitter while they went out to dinner or to play cards with other couples.

Most of their energies and concern during the past two months had been concentrated on their son. It was recommended that they also devote some additional time to their two-year-old daughter. This was a stressful time for her, too! Since her mother and father could not give her their sole attention, she would be competing for time with her new brother, and the feelings of sibling rivalry would emerge. She would need to feel that her position in the family was also unique and important—that is, a daughter and their first born. Time should be planned for her to have some activities with her parents. This would emphasize that she was "old" enough to be included in their activities.

They were warned to expect some acting-out behavior and possibly some regressive behavior in her bids for "equal" attention.

During their last visit Laura and Peter were assured they could return to the Center if they felt the need for help with a problem.

Summation of the paradigm

This case study concerned a young mother unable to cope with problems of an unexpectedly premature baby. Assessment of the stressful events precipitating the crisis indicated that Laura regarded herself as a failure for not delivering a full-term baby. This was reinforced by the criticisms of her mother-in-law and the lack of situational support from her husband.

In the assessment phase the therapist maintained focus on the immediate area of stress that could have precipitated the crisis. After determining a possible cause-effect relationship, a goal for intervention was established. Laura was encouraged to ventilate her feelings of guilt and inadequacy in the present situation. Realistic perception of the event developed as the therapist provided information leading to an intellectual understanding of the relationship between the event and the resulting symptoms of stress. The husband was brought in as a situational support, and new as well as previously successful coping skills were utilized in resolving the crisis.

STATUS AND ROLE CHANGE
Theoretical concepts

Throughout his life the individual is constantly in the process of joining and leaving social groups related to family, occupation, recreation, education, church, and so forth. *Status* within each of these groups is determined by the relative rights and duties that society assigns to the position. *Role* is determined by the expectations of society that the individual will carry out the duties of his position. If the member's position is changed within the group, his status and role will also change (Linton, 1956).

Allport[5] cites four interrelated meanings of the term role. The first, *role expectation,* is what society expects of the individual. *Role conception* means *how* the individual perceives the effect of the role upon his self-concept. He defines the role according to his perception and his needs, which are influenced by life goals, basic values, and congruency with other roles he is expected to perform. *Role acceptance,* like role conception, is a highly subjective matter. Not all roles are willingly accepted, nor are they willingly altered. The political process is one example of the kind of pressure that society can exert to force a role change. Reciprocal role changes will occur for all dependent upon the winner's (and loser's) new status.

Role performance depends upon role expectation, conception, and acceptance. The performance of the role will meet the expectations of society only to the degree that there has been mutual communication and understanding throughout the process. The greater the disagreement in any area of understanding, the greater the possibility of failure in the performance.

A person tends to perceive a role from his view of how it relates to his self-concept. The "self" might be defined as the image that the individual builds of himself through interpretation of what he thinks others are judging him to be. It is also derived from the reflected values that others place upon him and the values that he places upon himself in his societal roles. As new evaluations are perceived, he is obliged to reconcile these new concepts with preexisting ones. Increasing conflictual appraisals of the self result in increased tension and anxiety, leading to a state of disequilibrium.

A person tries to avoid accepting a role that might threaten the security of his self-concept. Various defensive mechanisms are used to escape conflict and to ensure the integrity of self. Danger occurs when an unacceptable change in role is forced by society and cannot be avoided. For example, in the sudden death of a husband, the existing role of wife ceases to exist; the position is gone and its status with it. Without a husband there is no wife role. Similar loss situations may occur in occupations and other groups; a business closes or a position is abolished so the need for certain roles no longer exists.

The individual's feelings of loss are in accordance with the value that he places on the role. Effects of the loss are viewed in relation to the self-image, and this involves consideration of the negative factors that might cause conflicting appraisals from others. The greater the conflict between self-concept and expectations due to role change, the more painful is the decision-making experience.

---

[5]Allport, Gordon W.: Pattern and growth in personality, New York, 1961, Holt, Rinehart & Winston, Inc., p. 184.

Changes in roles related to loss of status are particularly critical because they represent a direct threat to self-esteem and may encourage the development of a negative self-concept. If defensive coping mechanisms (such as projection or rationalization) prove ineffective in protecting the integrity of the self, anxiety and tension will rise and the balance of equilibrium will be disturbed.

The following case study illustrates a depressive reaction to a negative change in role status and loss of self-esteem. It was important in the initial interview to determine if Mr. E. was suicidal before intervention was initiated. Intervention focused on clarifying the problem area and assisting him to explore and ventilate unrecognized feelings. The therapist acted as situational support until other supports could be found in his environment.

Case study: Status and role change
Assessment of the individual and his problem

Mr. E. requested help at a crisis intervention center on the advice of his attorney. He was in a state of severe depression and anxiety. He described his symptoms as insomnia, inability to concentrate, and feelings of hopelessness and failure. He was a well-dressed man, 47 years old, who looked older than his stated age because of tense posture, a dull, depressed facial expression, and a rather flat, low tone of voice. Married for twenty-two years, he had three children, a girl 13 years old and two boys 8 and 10 years old.

His symptoms had begun about three weeks previously when his company closed their West Coast branch and he lost his job. His symptoms had increased in intensity during the past two days to the point where he remained in his room, lying in bed and not eating. He became frightened of his depressed thoughts and feared losing complete control of his actions.

During the initial session he stated to the therapist that he had never been without a job before. Immediately following graduation from college, twenty-two years before, he had started his own advertising agency in New York City. It had expanded over the years, and he had incorporated, retaining controlling interest and the position of company president. On several occasions he had been approached by larger companies with merger proposals. About a year ago one of the "top three" advertising companies offered him the presidency of a new West Coast branch, which he could run with full autonomy, gaining a great increase in prestige and salary. All expenses were to be paid for his family's move to the West Coast.

Mr. E. saw this as a chance to "make it big"—an opportunity that might never come his way again. His wife and children, however, did not share his enthusiasm. Mrs. E. had always lived in New York City and objected to his giving up his business where he was "really the boss." She liked the structured security of their life and did not want to leave it for one that she thought would be alien to her. The children sided with her, adding personal objections of their own. They had known only city life, had always gone to the same schools, and did not want to

Fig. 4. Case study: Mr. E.

move "way out West." Despite resistance from his family, he made the decision to accept the job offer. His business friends admired his decision to take the chance and expressed full confidence in his ability to succeed. Selling out his shares in his own company to his partner, he moved West with his family within a month.

In keeping with his new economic status and the prestige of his job, he leased a large home in an exclusive residential area. He left most of the responsibility for settling his family to his wife and became immediately involved in the organization of his new business. He described her reaction to the change as being "everything negative that she told me it would be." The children disliked their schools, made few friends, and did not seem to adjust to the pace of their peer group activities. His wife could not find housekeeping help to her liking and consequently felt tied down with work in the home. She missed her friends and clubs, was unable to find shops to satisfy her, and was constantly making negative comparisons between their present life style and their previous one. He felt that there had been a loss of communication between them. His present work was foreign to her, and he could not understand why she was having so many problems just because they had moved to a new location. Her attitude was one of constantly blaming everything that went wrong upon his decision to move West and into a new job.

About a month ago the company suddenly lost four big accounts. Although none of these losses had been a result of his management, immediate retrenchment in nationwide operations was necessary to save the company as a whole. The decision was made to close the newest branch office—his branch on the West Coast. There was no similar position available in the remaining offices, and he was offered a lesser position and salary in the Midwest. He was given two months in which to close out his office and to make a decision.

Mrs. E.'s attitude toward these sudden events was a quick "I told you so." She blamed him for their being "stranded out here without friends and a job." He said that he was not a bit surprised by her reaction and had expected it. He had been able to "tune out" her constant complaints in the past months because he had been so occupied by his job, but now he was forced to join her in making plans for his family's future and in considering their tenous economic status. He felt that he had been able to hold up pretty well under the dual pressures of closing out the business and planning for his family's future security. A week ago his wife had found a smaller home that would easily fit into their projected budget during the interim until he decided on a new job. He had felt a sense of relief that she had calmed down and was "working *with* me for a change."

Two days ago, however, their present landlord had sent a lawyer, threatening a lawsuit if Mr. E. broke the lease on their present home. His wife became hysterical, blaming him for signing such a lease and calling him a self-centered failure who had ruined his family's lives. "Suddenly I felt as though the bottom had fallen out of my world. I felt frozen and couldn't think what to do next, where to go, and who to ask for help. My family, my employees, everyone was blaming me for this mess! Maybe it *was* all my fault."

Until now, Mr. E. had always experienced a series of successes in his business and home life. Minor setbacks were usually anticipated and overcome with little need for him to seek outside guidance from others. Now, for the first time, he felt helpless to cope with a stressful situation alone. The threat of having to fulfill the lease on a house he could no longer afford not only destroyed his plans for his family, but also broke off what little support he had been receiving from his wife. His feelings of guilt and hopelessness were reinforced by the reality of the threatened lawsuit and the loss of situational support.

Planning of therapeutic intervention

Because of his total involvement in his new work Mr. E. had withdrawn from his previous business and family supports. The sudden loss of his job threatened him with role change and loss of status for which he had no previous coping experiences. Perceiving himself as a self-made success in the past, he now perceived himself as a self-made failure, both in business and in his parent-husband roles.

When asked by the therapist about his successful coping methods in the past, he said that he had always had recourse to discussions with his business friends. He now felt ashamed to contact them, "to let them know I've failed." He had always felt free to discuss home problems with his wife, and they usually had resolved them together. Now he seemed no longer able to communicate at home with his wife. When questioned if he was planning to kill himself he said "No, I could never take *that* way out. That never entered my mind." After determining that there was no threat of immediate suicide, the therapist initiated intervention.

Intervention

One goal of intervention was to assist Mr. E. in exploring unrecognized feelings about his change in role and status. His loss of situational supports and lack of available coping mechanisms for dealing with the present stressful situation were recognized as areas in need of attention.

In the next four weeks, through direct questioning, he began to see the present crisis as a reflection of his past business and family roles. Mr. E. had perceived himself as being a strong, independent "self-made" man in the past, feeling secure in his roles as "boss," husband, and father. He now felt shame at having to depend upon others for help in these roles. Coping experiences and skills learned in the past were proving to be inadequate in dealing with the sudden, unexpected, novel changes in his social orbit. The loss of situational support from his wife had added to his already high level of tension and anxiety. This resulted in the failure of what coping skills he had been using with marginal success, and in precipitation of the crisis.

After the fourth session, Mr. E.'s depression and feelings of hopelessness had diminished. His perception of the total situation had become more realistic, and he realized that the closing of the branch office was not due to any failure on his part. It was, in fact, the same decision that he thought he would have made had he been in charge of the overall operation. He further recognized what great importance he had placed on the possibility that this job would have been his "last chance to make it big." His available coping skills had not lessened in value but had, in fact, been increased by the experience of the situation.

By the fifth week Mr. E. had made significant changes in his situation, both in business and in his family life. He had been able to explore his attitudes about always feeling the need to be "the boss" and a sense of shame in being dependent upon others for support in decision making. He was now able to perceive the stressful events realistically and to cope with his anxieties.

He met with his former landlord and resolved the impending lawsuit, breaking the lease with amicable agreement on both sides. His family had already decided to move into a smaller home, and his wife and children were actively involved with the planning. He had contacted business friends in the East and accepted one of several offers for a lesser position. He would return East alone, his family choosing to follow later when he had reestablished himself. His wife and children made this choice rather than repeat the sudden move into an unsettled situation as they had a year ago.

He felt pride that his friends had competed for his services rather than giving him the "I told you so" that he had been dreading.

Anticipatory planning

Before termination Mr. E. and the therapist reviewed the adjustments and the tremendous progress Mr. E. had made in such a short period of time. It was emphasized that it had taken a great deal of strength for him to resolve such an extremely ego-shattering experience. He was also complimented on his ability to recognize the factors he could change, those he would be unable to change, and his new status in life.

He viewed the experience as having been very disturbing at the time, but felt he had gained a great deal of insight from it. He believed that he would be able to cope more realistically if a similar situation occurred in the future. He was quite pleased with his ability to extricate himself from a seemingly impossible situation.

In discussing his plans for the future, he stated that he no longer believed he had lost his chance for future advancement. He was realistic about past happenings and the possibility that such a crisis could occur again. He was relieved about his family's rapid adjustment to the lesser status of his new position. They were happy to be returning to family and friends on the East Coast.

He expressed optimism about again rising to a high position in business, concluding with, "I wonder if I could ever really settle for less?"

Summation of the paradigm

Mr. E.'s crisis was precipitated by a sudden change in role status (loss of his job) and threatened economic, social, and personal losses. Assessment of the crisis situation determined that he was depressed but not suicidal. Because he was overwhelmed by a sense of failure in both business and family roles, his perceptions of the events were distorted. Having no previous experience with personal failure of this scope, he was unable to cope with his feelings of guilt and depression. His wife's actions reinforced his low self-esteem, and she withdrew as situational support.

Realistic perception of the event developed as the therapist assisted him in exploring and ventilating unrecognized feelings; he was able to gain insight into relationships between his symptoms of depression and the stressful events. Mrs. E. resumed her role of situational support as his new coping skills were successfully implemented in resolving the crisis.

EXPERIMENTATION WITH LSD
Theoretical concepts

Almost any drug, if taken in sufficient quantity by a person sensitive to its effects, can produce a delirium. This is a confused state marked by disorientation, delusional thinking, and hallucinations. Other dimensions of awareness are possible, ranging from profound feelings of mystical union to terrifying convictions of madness and from ecstasy to despair. Drugs that produce such effects have many names: pseudohallucinogen, psychotomimetic (a mimicker of psychosis), mysticomimetic (mystical states), or psychedelic (mind manifesting).[6] One such drug that is creating much controversy and concern is lysergic acid diethylamide (LSD).

With the widespread, uncontrolled use of LSD, effects of the drug severe enough to require medical attention are seen frequently. In the United States neither LSD nor any similar drug, such as mescaline, peyote, psilocybin, and dimethyltryptamine (DMT), can be sold legally. The only legitimate source of supply of LSD is the National Institute of Mental Health. There is, however, a flourishing black market that readily supplies those desiring it. Since chemists (even amateur ones) can manufacture it with little difficulty, it can be cheaply and easily made.

Illicit LSD is usually supplied in capsules or on sugar cubes, with the amount of the drug in each dose varying greatly. It is tasteless, odorless, colorless, and water soluble. Within about thirty minutes after oral ingestion, sympathomimetic symptoms occur, which are characterized by dilation of the pupils, nausea, flushing, and chilliness. Shortly thereafter the psychedelic effects begin. These consist of change of mood, generally in the direction of euphoria but occasionally toward depression, distortion of sensory perception (usually visual), distortions of body image, depersonalization, increased vividness of fantasy, and hallucinations.

LSD is often taken by many who believe it can give an instant psychoanalysis

---

[6]Cohen, Sidney: The beyond within; the LSD story, New York, 1966, Atheneum Publishers, pp. 12-13.

or who are motivated by the desire to have a mystical or religious experience. Most individuals who try LSD are ones who have had experiences with other drugs, such as marijuana, "reds," "bennies," "magic mushroom," and so forth.

The most obvious danger from the use of LSD is to those who are emotionally unstable. The effects of a single dose usually last from eight to ten hours, and the experience, or "trip," may recur in some individuals without any further ingestion of LSD. During the experience, the person is in an emotionally precarious condition and might panic. The panic may take any form and in certain instances may result in a need for hospitalization due to a psychotic break or for extensive psychotherapy. LSD use may also permit the release of repressed fears of homosexuality, death, insanity, and so forth into conscious awareness. While in panic, the individual may hurt himself or others in an effort to protect himself from imagined attack. The drug may impair judgment, and users have been known to disrobe publicly, drive dangerously, and act upon such grandiose delusions that they can fly or stop a speeding car with their hands.

Panic or psychotic reactions caused by LSD have been successfully treated with a phenothiazine such as chlorpromazine, usually given intramuscularly. Because a person under its influence may be in a state of extreme hypersensitivity, a calm, safe environment is needed to allay some of the fears.

The following case study illustrates one individual's reaction to the use of LSD. The initial assessment was made by the therapist during a telephone conversation in which it was learned that the use of LSD was involved. Tom was reexperiencing a "bad trip" and was in an emotionally precarious condition due to panic. The immediate concern of the therapist was getting Tom in for help, relieving his panic state with medication, and sustaining him until he was more stable. Intervention was planned to give him accurate information and an intellectual understanding of the effects of LSD. Opportunity was provided for him to explore and ventilate his underlying feelings of depression and inadequacy.

Case study: LSD
Assessment of the individual and his problem

Tom, a young college student, contacted a crisis intervention center by telephone, saying he knew he "was going to die; I can't control it . . . I must!" He denied the receptionist's repeated requests for more information and kept repeating, "I need help, or I'll die!" Attempts to elicit information about where he was and how he was going to die were answered by desperate sounds of sobbing and saying, "I don't know . . . I don't know." After the second telephone call he was connected directly to a therapist. While attempting to extract more information, the therapist discerned that Tom was confused and disoriented and suspected the use of drugs. When questioned about the use of drugs, Tom stated that a week ago he had taken LSD but had not taken any drugs since. He added that he had had "a bad trip; I feel the same way now . . . I'm so depressed . . . life isn't worth living. I've

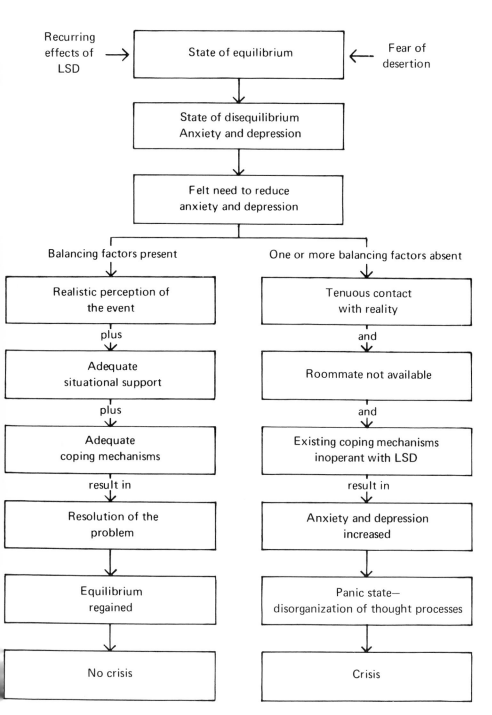

Fig. 5. Case study: Tom.

tried three times to jump out of the window of the dorm, but I can't do it . . . but I know I will!" When asked where he was, he said he was in a telephone booth (approximately two blocks from the center). The therapist very specifically told him how to reach the center and emphasized that she would be waiting for him.

Tom arrived ten minutes later and, because of the urgency of the situation, bypassed the usual admission procedure and was seen immediately by the therapist. He exhibited a high state of anxiety and was almost incoherent. The therapist managed to secure information as to age, residence, friends, family, and so on. When Tom explained about his trip on LSD a week ago and that he was feeling "the same way now," he was reassured that it was possible he was "reliving" the previous experience. A medical consultation was arranged, and he received medication. His roommate, Jake, was contacted and came immediately. In approximately thirty minutes Tom was calmer, although still confused, and he did not reiterate his previous wish to die. He still found it difficult to believe that he could be reexperiencing his previous trip. The therapist thought that he could go home with his roommate, since Jake was aware of the situation and felt able to cope with Tom's feelings and behavior. Jake was given medication to sustain Tom and the twenty-four-hour emergency telephone number, and an appointment was made for Tom to return for therapy.

Planning of therapeutic intervention

The therapist utilized Jake to gain more knowledge about Tom's previous experience with drugs and his habitual patterns of coping with stress.

Jake stated that both he and Tom had tried "pot" a few times but did not use it regularly because it "didn't turn us on." They had also tried "reds" and "bennies"—just "to see what it was like." When questioned about the LSD experience, he stated that about a week ago Tom had come to their room at the dorm with two other students who had LSD with them. They offered some to Tom and Jake after describing their "really great experience" with LSD. Jake refused and advised Tom not to try it. Tom rebelled and said, "It might be fun to try it." When Tom began to feel the effects of the drug, he apparently became frightened and panicked. He kept repeating, "I want to die . . . I must die . . . I'm not fit to live!" He began crying and asking Jake to help him. After the effects wore off, Jake tried to get Tom to talk about what had happened but he refused. He acted depressed and began withdrawing from social contacts and school activities, cutting classes and staying in the dorm, usually just lying in bed and staring at the ceiling.

When questioned about what had occurred immediately prior to Tom's called to the center, Jake said that earlier he had tried to talk to Tom about his strange behavior. Tom became angry and told him to "leave me alone . . . you don't understand . . . get lost!" Jake left the dorm and went to a movie; he had just returned when he was called by the therapist.

When asked about Tom's previous patterns of interaction and reacting to stress, he stated that Tom was a "real nice guy," usually an A or B student and very active socially and in school activities. He said Tom was constantly busy and that he felt that he really pushed to avoid being alone. They had roomed together for two years, and Jake thought that basically Tom was a very lonely person because all of his relationships seemed superficial. He believed that he was the only real friend Tom had at school and that Tom usually accepted his decisions and opinions when he was undecided about what to do. It was thought that Jake would be an available situational support for Tom. The crisis-precipitating event was apparently the quarrel with Jake and the fear that he had been deserted.

Intervention

Tom needed to gain information and intellectual understanding of the effects of LSD; he also needed an opportunity to express his feelings of depression and inadequacy.

When Tom returned to the therapist the following week, he was calm and his perception and thinking were clear, his affect was flattened, and he spoke in a low, even tone. He slumped in the chair and expressed the desire for "help" because "I'm so depressed." When asked to be more specific, he said he could not—"I just feel so dead, I can't really put my finger on any one thing."

When questioned about experiences with LSD, he paled noticeably and looked anxious. He stated that he did not want to discuss it—"It was horrible . . . a nightmare . . . I want to forget it." He refused to discuss what he had experienced. In subsequent sessions he still refused to discuss his LSD experiences but was able to express some of his feelings about his depressive state. He admitted that he was basically a lonely person and that he used "busy" activities to avoid being alone. At the fourth session he appeared extremely anxious; he was perspiring and chain smoking and stated that he wanted to discuss his trip and that he was unable to sleep the night before because he felt that he might have the experience again.

What had frightened him the most was the feeling that he was standing outside his own body, looking back at it; all he could see was "a hollow shell . . . a nothing." The feeling was so strong that "I realized it must be true; I am nothing . . . just a hollow shell! I had no reason to live—I wanted to die." It was explained that this could occur in an LSD experience, but recurrence of the feelings without reingesting LSD was not common. He was reassured that if he did not use LSD again, the feelings would probably diminish. Apparently the ability to verbalize his feelings provided a catharsis for Tom, and his anxiety and tension decreased.

In the next sessions his feelings of depression remained, although they had lessened somewhat in intensity. He was able to discuss them freely with the therapist and at the dorm with Jake.

Anticipatory planning

During the termination session, Tom and the therapist discussed the advisability of his continuing in longer-term therapy. Tom stated that he felt he was just beginning to recognize and understand his feelings of depression, and wanted more help. He was referred outside the center for longer-term therapy.

Addendum

Approximately a year and a half later Tom returned to the center for a visit. He was in graduate school and engaged to be married. He stated that he was still in therapy, "was feeling great," and "no longer felt the need to experiment with drugs."

Summation of the paradigm

Tom's precarious level of emotional stability after a bad trip with LSD was dangerously lowered by the quarrel with Jake and his feelings of desertion by his only friend.

His unrealistic perception of the event was due to his tenuous contact with reality, and lack of available situational supports precipitated a crisis. Reaction to the release of repressed fears and feelings while experiencing the effects of LSD apparently caused him to panic. His thought processes became disorganized, and he was unable to function. Intervention was fourfold. First, immediate intervention was needed to reduce Tom's panic and intense anxiety, a medical consultation was arranged, medication was given, and a situational support was contacted. The next phase of intervention was focused on obtaining knowledge about Tom, his previous experience with drugs, and his usual pattern of coping with stress. After this phase Tom was given accurate information and assisted to gain an understanding of the effects of LSD. Time was then spent in helping him to explore his feelings of depression and inadequacy.

PHYSICAL ILLNESS
Theoretical concepts

Diseases are known to have their places, as well as their times. Primitive societies have been characterized by health problems related to recurrent famines, and urban societies, until recently, by epidemics of infectious disease. Modern industrial societies are characterized by a new set of diseases: obesity, arteriosclerosis, hypertension, diabetes and widespread symptoms of anxiety. Arising from these are two of the three greatest disablers and killers of our own place and time: coronary heart disease and stroke. In recent years increasing concern has focused investigation not only on the etiology and epidemiology of cardiac disease, but on factors affecting the process of recovery.

The unexpected recognition that one has heart disease is usually a crisis event for an individual. The disease could also be a chronic condition, persisting throughout life and precipitating a series of crises both for the patient and his family.

The conceptualization of the recovery process in heart disease as a response to crisis provides strategic advantages in approaching the problem. It leads to focusing on the kinds of adaptive and maladaptive mechanisms that patients employ in coping with this illness, on the stages of recovery, and on the resources that patients use and require at each stage. Viewing response to coronary heart disease as a problem that can be approached through crisis intervention permits the utilization of concepts and formulations inherent in crisis theory.

In a discussion of the rehabilitation of patients with cardiac disease, a report by the World Health Organization in 1966 distinguishes between phases of the recovery process in terms of time and coping tasks. The first phase is categorized as one in which the patient spends approximately three weeks in bed, with minimal physical activity. In the next phase the patient spends approximately six weeks at home with a variety of sedentary activities. In the third phase, which lasts from three to six months, the patient makes a gradual reentry into the occupational world.

Lee and Bryner (1961) conceptualize phases according to the kinds of care the physician must provide for the patient at each point of the process. They specify (1) evaluation of the patient and his environment, (2) management of the patient, and (3) reestablishment of the patient in his community.

In other formulations of recovery phases, emphasis is on the kinds of therapeutic or rehabilitative relationships that predominate at each point. Hellerstein and Goldstone (1954) describe the first, or acute, phase as one in which the relationship between the doctor and patient is of the utmost importance. The convalescent phase then follows, with the relationship between the patient and his family and friends becoming primary. During the recovery, or third, phase the employer or vocational counselor becomes the vital participant in the rehabilitation of the patient with cardiac disease.

Phases have also been viewed in terms of the emotional adaptation of the patient. Kubie (1955) suggests that a first phase is marked by initial shock, and the second by appreciation of the full extent of the disability. In the third there is "recovery from the lure of hospital care," and in the fourth and final phase there is "a facing of independent, unsupported, competitive life."

Among the most obvious and critical determinants of the outcome of the recovery process are the severity of heart damage, the degree of impairment, and the physiological resources of the patient. While cardiac damage has much to do with setting limits on performance and affecting levels of adjustment, studies of physiological factors alone contribute only partially to understanding the recovery process. Research on the importance of the premorbid personality of the patient as a determinant of adjustment to illness suggests that this is a second important factor in the recovery process.

Other important factors bearing on the recovery process include the various psychological mechanisms that the patient uses in handling his illness. If the recovery process is viewed as a response to a crisis situation, then the individual mechanisms used by patients appear particularly important in the resolution of the crisis. The significance of emotional response to disease has often been underlined in discussing the elements that determine recovery. McIver (1960) states, "The way in which a crisis is handled emotionally may significantly influence the eventual outcome of a case in terms of the extent of recovery and the degree of rehabilitation achieved." Reiser (1951) emphasizes that it is essential to deal with the anxieties associated with the diagnosis and symptoms of heart disease if the therapy of cardiac disease is to attain its optimal effect.

A common view held is that during the acute phase of any serious illness the patient's emotional state is characterized by fear, since the illness threatens his total integrity as well as his sense of personal adequacy and worth to others.

Compared with other serious illnesses, heart disease has several unique features. Associated as it is with sudden death, it is viewed by the patient and his family as an immediate and severe threat to life. Hollender (1958) has written that even in the most stable patients the onset of heart disease is associated with an onslaught of anxiety. During the first days of illness the patient with heart disease must assume a passive role, and some believe that this tends to compound his anxiety. Physical restriction usually increases feelings of helplessness, vulnerability, and depression. The patient is then handicapped in utilizing defense mechanisms that should ultimately help him to adjust to his altered status.

Although coping responses vary widely, there appears to be a core of relatively uniform responses of adjustment. For example, depression and regression have often been reported as the initial reaction to the illness. Some patients display aggression and hostility, placing the blame for the illness on external factors. Some deal with the threat to life by denial of the illness.

It has been suggested that certain coping responses are appropriate at one stage of recovery but are inappropriate at another. When patients at the same stage of recovery are compared, similar responses may function in different ways: constructively for some patients but hindering recovery for others. There is disagreement at present as to the role denial plays in recovery. Some regard denial, which may lead to noncooperation with the physician, as a response of self-destruction. Others consider that denial arises from a belief in the integrity of the self and the invulnerability of the body. It is regarded as constructive and associated with the maintenance of health.

Since each patient will react as an individual in this life-threatening situation, it would be well to remember that the therapist will, in all probability, see a variety of coping responses being utilized. It is not the therapist's role to change the patient's pattern of coping, but to understand that his reaction to his illness is part of his defense.

King (1962) has stated that "Man's basis for action in health and disease is a composite of many things. One crucial variable is the way that he sees or perceives the situation . . . and all of the social ramifications that accompany it." These perceptions are conditioned by socialization in a sociocultural context. How the patient responds to the disease is influenced by what he has learned. The content of the learning is in turn determined by the norms and values of the society in which he lives. The meaning of the disease, his attitude toward medical practitioners, his willingness to comply with medical advice, and his management of his life after a heart attack are all influenced by the attitudes and beliefs that he has learned.

Pertinent to the recovery process is the conceptualization of the "sick role," which Parsons (1951) describes as a social role, with its own culturally defined rights and obligations. While a person may be physiologically ill, he is not recognized as legitimately ill unless his illness fulfills the criteria or standards set by the society. Once defined as legitimately able to be in the "sick role," he is expected to meet certain expectations of others. He is expected, for example, to make an effort toward becoming well and to seek help. In turn he has the right to expect certain kinds of behavior in others toward him, including a willingness to permit him to relinquish his normal social role responsibilities.

Willingness to accept the sick role may mean that a patient with heart disease is likely to follow the regimen of his physician and to care for himself in ways that will maximize his recovery. At the same time, reluctance to accept the sick role may also influence the recovery process favorably. Such a patient may be anxious to avoid being defined as sick. Like the willing patient, he too may follow the therapeutic regimen in order to shorten the period of incapacity. On the other hand, reluctance to view himself as sick may lead a patient to comply minimally with medical advice and to attempt full activity before he is physically able to do so.

In essence, social and cultural standards and expectations may have a strong influence upon the kinds of action a patient with cardiac disease may take in regard to his own health status.

Case study: Physical illness

Mr. Z., aged 43, was chairing a board meeting of his large, successful manufacturing corporation when he developed shortness of breath, dizziness, and a crushing, vicelike pain in his chest. An ambulance was called, and he was taken to the medical center. Subsequently he was admitted to the coronary care unit with a diagnosis of impending myocardial infarction.

Mr. Z. was married, with three children: Steve, aged 14; Sean, aged 12; and Liza, aged 8. He was president and the majority stockholder of a large manufacturing corporation. He had no previous history of cardiovascular problems, although his father had died at the age of 38 of a massive coronary occlusion. His oldest brother had died at the age of 42 from the same condition; and his other brother, still living, was a semiinvalid after suffering two heart attacks—one at the age of 44 and the other at the age of 47.

Mr. Z. was tall, slim, suntanned, and very athletic. He swam daily, jogged every morning for thirty minutes, played golf regularly, and was an avid sailor who participated in every yacht regatta, usually winning. He was very health conscious and had annual physical checkups, watched his diet, and quit smoking to avoid

Fig. 6. Case study: Mr. Z.

possible damage to his heart, determined to avoid dying young or becoming an invalid like his brother.

When he was admitted to the coronary care unit he was conscious. Though in a great deal of pain, he seemed determined to control his own fate. While in the coronary care unit he was an exceedingly difficult patient, a trial to the nursing staff and his physician. He constantly watched and listened to everything going on around him and demanded complete explanations about any procedure, equipment, or medication he received. He would sleep in brief naps, and only when he was totally exhausted. Despite his obvious tension and anxiety, his condition stabilized. The damage to his heart was considered minimal, and his prognosis was good. As the pain diminished, he began asking when he could go home and when he could go back to work. He was impatient to be moved to a private room so he could conduct some of his business by telephone.

Mr. Z. denied having any anxiety or concerns about his condition, although his behavior on the unit contradicted his denial. Recognizing that Mr. Z. was coping inappropriately with the stress of illness, his physician requested as consultant a therapist whose expertise was crisis intervention to work with Mr. Z., to help him through the crisis period.

The therapist agreed to work with Mr. Z. for one hour a week for six weeks. Their first session was scheduled the second day of his stay in the coronary care unit.

Assessment of the individual and his problem

The therapist reviewed Mr. Z.'s chart and talked with his physician prior to the first session in order to gain an accurate assessment of Mr. Z.'s physical condition and to gain some knowledge of factors (socioeconomic status, marital status, family history, and so on) to assist in assessing his biopsychosocial needs.

In the first session the therapist observed Mr. Z.'s overt and covert signs of anxiety and depression and determined, through discussion with him, his perception of what hospitalization meant to him, his usual patterns of coping with stress, and available situational supports. Through direct questions and reflective verbal feedback she was able to elicit the reasons for his behavior and reactions to his illness and to his confinement in the coronary care unit.

Observing his suntanned, youthful appearance and the general physical condition of a very active and persistent athlete, the therapist questioned him about his life style and patterns prior to his hospitalization. Mr. Z. was quite adamant about his "minor" condition and the possibility of curtailed activity. He stated that he was very aware of his family's tendency toward cardiac conditions, but added, "I have always taken excellent care of myself to avoid the possibility of becoming a cardiac cripple like my brother." Apparently he was not too concerned about the prospect of dying; in fact, he might prefer it to the overwhelming prospect of being a useless, dependent invalid.

He expressed concern about the length of time he might have to spend in the hospital. When questioned about his concern he stated: "I *have* to be in good shape by the second of December [approximately three and a half months]: I've entered the big yacht race, and I plan to win again!"

When he was asked how his wife and children were reacting to his illness and hospitalization, Mr. Z.'s facial expression and general body tension relaxed noticeably. He smiled and said, "My wife, Ann, is simply unbelievable; she takes everything in stride. She is always cool, calm, and collected. She even met with the board of directors and told them to delay any major decisions until I return—but that any minor decisions she could handle!"

The therapist asked if she could meet his wife. Mr. Z. replied that his wife would be in to see him soon and suggested she stay and meet her.

After meeting with them briefly, the therapist asked Mrs. Z. to stop by her office before leaving.

Session with Mrs. Z. Mrs. Z. arrived at the office and sank gratefully into a chair, losing the bright, cheerful, and optimistic manner she had maintained while with her husband. Observing her concerned expression and slumped posture, the therapist inquired, "You are very concerned about your husband, aren't you?" Mrs. Z. readily admitted that she was concerned but did not want her husband to know. When asked what specifically concerned her, she replied: "Jim's inability to accept any type of forced inactivity and his refusal to accept the possibility that he might have to change his hectic life style. He can't *bear* the thought of being ill or being dependent upon anyone or anything!"

The therapist explained that it is difficult for many patients to accept a passive, dependent role while ill and that it takes time for them to adjust to a changed life style. She then explained to Mrs. Z. that the physician had arranged for Mr. Z. to have therapy sessions for the next six weeks to help him through his crisis. Mrs. Z. seemed relieved that someone else recognized the problems confronting her husband and would help him as he worked through his feelings about his illness and unwanted, though inevitable, change in life style.

The therapist suggested that Mrs. Z. might also need some support, as she too had to adjust to Mr. Z.'s illness. They agreed to meet for an hour each week so they could work together toward a resolution of the crisis. A convenient time was arranged each week when Mrs. Z. came to visit her husband.

Planning of therapeutic intervention

Mr. Z.'s denial of the possibility that he might die like his father and oldest brother or that he might become an invalid, "useless and dependent," like his other brother was considered of prime importance. It was felt that the first goal of intervention was to assist Mr. Z. to ventilate his feelings about his illness and hospitalization. A second goal was to assist him to perceive the event realistically. A third goal established was that of giving support to Mrs. Z. and assisting her in coping with the stress induced by her husband's hospitalization.

Intervention

It was felt that Mr. Z.'s high anxiety level would interfere with his ability to express his feelings about his illness and his hospitalization. In an attempt to reduce his anxiety, the therapist made two recommendations to his physician, which were accepted. The first recommendation was that Mr. Z. be moved out of the coronary care unit to a private room as soon as possible. The environmental surroundings in the coronary care unit, with its overwhelming and complex equipment, strange sounds, and constant activities of the staff, apparently increased Mr. Z.'s anxiety. Because of the stressful situation, he was not getting sufficient rest. After his move to a private room later that afternoon, he began to relax noticeably, became much less demanding of the staff, and began sleeping and eating better.

The second recommendation was that he be permitted to use the telephone for thirty minutes three times a day. Thus he was able to conduct some of his business from his bed. This apparently made him feel less dependent, and the increased mental activity relieved some of his anxiety about becoming a "helpless" invalid.

In the next sessions Mr. Z. began to discuss—hesitantly at first, and then more freely—his feelings about his illness and his reaction to hospitalization. He discussed his father's sudden death when he was in his teens and how lost he would have felt if his older brother had not stepped in and taken over. All three brothers were very close, and the death of the oldest one, while Mr. Z. was in college, reactivated the grievous loss he had felt for his father. He was just beginning to accept his oldest brother's death when, a year later, his other brother had a severe heart attack and was unable to continue in the family business. As Mr. Z. saw it, his brother was a "helpless" invalid. Mr. Z., the youngest son, then became the major stockholder and president of the corporation.

He stated that while he certainly didn't *want* to die, he was less afraid of dying than he was of becoming useless, helpless, and a burden to his family.

Through discussion and verbal feedback, it was possible to get Mr. Z. to view his illness and the changes it would make in his life in a realistic perspective: No, he was *not* an invalid. Yes, he *would* be able to work and live a *normal* life. No, he would *not* have to give up sailing, just have someone else do most of the crewing. Yes, he *would* be able to resume his activities but would continue them at a more leisurely pace: instead of scheduling fifteen things to do in one day, schedule seven and a half, and so. Gradually he became more accepting as he began to realize that the impending myocardial infarction was a warning he should heed and that with proper care and some diminishing of his usual hectic pace he could continue to live a productive and useful life.

The therapist continued to meet with Mrs. Z. to give her support and began anticipatory planning for her husband's convalescence at home. She discussed with her Mr. Z.'s strong need to feel independent and in control of all situations and encouraged her to continue to let her husband make decisions for the family. She assured Mrs. Z. that he would be able to continue a relatively normal life and that she did not need to protect and "coddle" him, something he would greatly resent! When asked how their children were reacting to their father's hospitalization, Mrs. Z. replied: "At first they were terribly concerned and silent; now they are beginning to ask, 'When is he coming home, and what can we do?' " It was obvious that Mr. Z. had strong situational support in his family!

Mr. Z.'s recovery progressed fairly smooth, and he began to ambulate and take care of his basic needs. While more accepting of his need for some assistance, he still became upset and impatient if the staff intervened to assist him in routine care.

Mr. Z. was discharged after the fourth week, with instructions for his convalescence at home. The therapist continued to meet with Mr. and Mrs. Z. at their home during the fifth and sixth weeks to assist the family toward stabilization as Mr. Z. adjusted to his new regimen of reduced activity and to provide anticipatory planning for their future.

Anticipatory planning

By the end of the fifth week, with the strong support of his family and the therapist, Mr. Z. was able to view his illness and his feelings about curtailing some of his hectic activities in a more accepting and realistic manner. His family still consulted him for advice and opinions regarding family decisions. This made him feel he was still an active, participating member of the family.

He was able to conduct a large part of his business from his home by having board meetings there and through periodic telephone conversations to his office. His secretary came to his home three days a week to take dictation and to secure his signature when needed on documents. Thus, he still remained in control of his business life, which contributed greatly to his self-esteem.

The children and Mrs. Z. were encouraged to continue in their usual daily activities so that Mr. Z. would not feel that his being at home was disrupting to their lives. It also helped Mrs. Z. to cope with her feelings and her desire to protect her husband from stress. Gradually she was able to realize that he was capable of coping with some stress and that he was not as fragile as she had believed him to be.

Before termination the therapist and Mr. Z. reviewed the adjustments he had made and the insights he had gained into his own behavior. He was able to intellectually understand his reasons for his denial and dependence/independence conflicts.

He was very optimistic about his future and felt that he could adjust to a reduced-activity schedule. He still, rather wistfully, was hoping his physician would approve his entering the yacht race.

He was realistic about his physical condition and the possibility that a coronary attack could occur again, stating, "At least now I've learned to relax and roll with the punches."

Mrs. Z. and the children felt that they would be able to cope with the occasional bouts of frustration and temper flare-ups of Mr. Z. They were now aware of how difficult it was for him to make the many adjustments necessary to his new way of life.

Addendum

Several months later the physician informed the therapist that he had permitted Mr. Z. to enter the yacht race, as a passenger, not as crew, and that his yacht had finished third.

DIVORCE
Theoretical concepts

In Western society, divorce has become a common rather than a rare occurrence. Much has been written and hypothesized about the causes and effects of divorce upon individuals and family members. An estimated 494,000 decrees of divorce or annulment were granted in the United States in 1966, as compared with an estimated 481,000 for 1965. This is an increase of 13,000, or 2.7%, the highest national divorce rate since 1953.[7] Since divorce rates are so high and many marriages are centers of friction and unhappiness, something must be lacking in the preparation for marriage. No event in life of equal importance is viewed with so little realism, and marriage seems to come about with little or no preparation.

Marriage and its demands upon individuals can be stressful, and failure to sustain a marriage can precipitate a crisis. Rapoport (1963) delineates three subphases of marriage when stress is the most common: the engagement, honeymoon, and early marriage. Engaged couples confront major tasks on two levels, intrapersonal and interpersonal. The intrapersonal task implies a review of readiness for marriage on a conscious, preconscious, or unconscious level of psychological maturity. This readiness will be affected by the individual needs of the person and by his perceived subcultural norms. The interpersonal tasks are concerned with developing and interpersonal adjustment or accomodation that will be satisfactory in the marital relationship. The engagement period involves a process of separation from previous life patterns and of commitment of the couple to one another. The honeymoon period is a time for establishing a basic sense of harmony. The early marriage phase (the first three months) involves establishing a system of authority, decision-making patterns, and patterns of sexual relationships.

It is evident that individuals do not always accomplish these necessary tasks in the first few months of marriage. For some it may easily extend into the first few years of marriage. Additional stress factors may occur in this period to create even greater disequilibrium.

The largest proportion of divorces occurs in the early years of marriage among childless couples. The peak period of divorces is in the second year of marriage, after which the rate drops rapidly. A number of factors, other than those previously mentioned, are precipitating causes of divorce. Among these are urban background, early marriage (15 to 19 years of age), short courtship, short engagement, mixed racial or religious marriages, disapproval of friends and relatives, dissimilar backgrounds, and unhappy parental marriages.

Today there is greater acceptance of the possibility of divorce; because of this acceptance, divorced persons have lost some of the feelings of failure and guilt that were formerly associated with it. The higher divorce rate may reflect new values placed on marriage. Marriage is no longer accepted as an "endurance race" that is doggedly maintained "for the sake of the children." The current demands

---

[7]Long, Luman H., editor: The world almanac and book of facts, New York, 1968, Newspaper Enterprise Association, Inc. p. 269.

are for a "good marriage," one that meets the needs of the individuals involved. Even from the point of view of the children, who seemingly pay the highest price for marital failure, divorce may in certain circumstances create fewer psychological problems if the children are not used as pawns by the separating parents.

The rate of remarriage after divorce is quite high, and in cases where both parties had been divorced two or more times the ratio climbs even higher. Greene (1968) assumes that divorce is a repetitive phenomenon. It is apparent that an unresolved neurotic pattern, carried over from one marriage to another, would tend to reinforce the individual's failure pattern in the subsequent marriage.

This case study[8] concerns a young woman, 23 years old, who sought help from a crisis center on the advice of her attorney because of an impending divorce. Neither Margie nor her husband had attained the psychological maturity or "readiness" necessary to enter marriage. Margie's impulsive marriages after brief courtships indicated her unrealistic expectations and attitudes toward marriage. Clues given in the assessment phase indicated that she felt herself a failure as a woman. These guilt feelings and lack of her usual situational supports precipitated a crisis. Intervention was planned to assist her to cope with her feelings of failure and guilt and to view her divorce in more realistic terms.

Case study: Divorce
Assessment of the individual and his problem

Margie, an extremely attractive young woman in the process of divorce from her third husband, was referred to a crisis intervention center for help because of severe depression and anxiety. This was manifested by insomnia, lack of appetite, tremulousness, inability to concentrate, and frequent crying spells. These symptoms had begun three weeks earlier when she was notified of the date of the divorce proceedings. She had lost her job because she was unable to control her crying spells and had subsequently developed bursitis in her shoulder, which further limited her ability to work. Her symptoms had intensified so much in the past three days that she felt she was losing complete control over her emotions and needed help.

During the initial session, Margie stated that she did not want a divorce and that she still loved her husband, even though he did not love her. When questioned about the increased intensity of symptoms that had begun three days ago, she stated that at that time she had been informed by her attorney that the only way she could receive alimony would be to countersue for divorce.

In Margie's previous two divorces she had remained a passive participant; her husbands had sued her for divorce. She had accepted these and had not contested. Now, for the first time, due to her inability to work she was forced to become an active participant in a divorce she did not want. She stated frequently that "some-

[8]Morley, Wilbur E., Messick, Janice M., and Aguilera, Donna C.: Crisis; paradigms of intervention, J. Psychiatr. Nurs. **5:**540-543, Nov.-Dec. 1967.

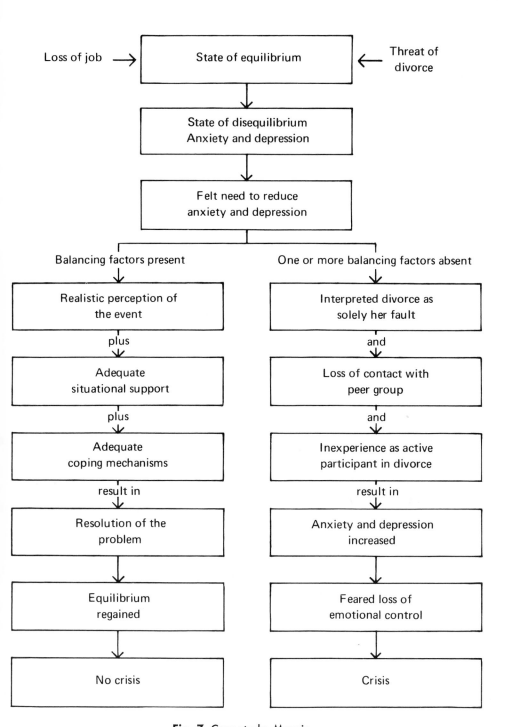

Fig. 7. Case study: Margie.

thing must be wrong with me if I can't hold a husband," and later commented, "I don't feel this is a good marriage—but I hate to fail again." This ambivalence and her expressed guilt feelings were felt to be part of the crisis-precipitating event, as was the necessity of being forced to take an active part in a divorce she did not want.

As a result of the assessment, the therapist thought that, although Margie was depressed and expressed feelings of worthlessness, she was not suicidal and did not constitute a threat to others.

Planning of therapeutic intervention

Margie had almost totally withdrawn from her social and family contacts. Her mother came occasionally to give her money for rent and bring her food. Beyond this social contact she remained isolated in the apartment she had previously shared with her husband, weeping at intervals, staring at her husband's picture, and unable to decide whether or not to contest the divorce.

Since she had not been forced into active decision making in her previous divorces, she had no coping experiences in this specific situation. When questioned about her previous methods of coping with stress, she stated that usually she had no problems because she remained involved in her work and its many social contacts, usually bowling and going to bars with friends. Her present inability to work eliminated these sources of social support, distractions from the problem, and her previous successful coping mechanisms could not be used.

The goal of intervention was established by the therapist to assist Margie to recognize and cope with her feelings of ambivalence and guilt. Unrecognized feelings about her marriage and the impending divorce were also to be explored.

Intervention

In the next three weeks, through direct questioning and reflection of verbal and nonverbal clues to Margie, it became possible for her to view the present crisis and its effect upon her in relationship to her previous marriages and divorces.

Margie wanted desperately to marry in order to become a housewife and mother. Her usual social contacts and previous patterns of meeting men (bowling alleys and bars) and her impulsive marriages (Las Vegas, three times) and reasons for marriage ("I thought I could help him . . . he needed me") were not meeting this need. The men she had met and married, and who later divorced her, were men who did not want to "settle down" with a wife and children. Instead, they wanted a gay, attractive companion to show off to their friends. Margie always hoped that they would change after marriage. However, they remained unchanged and divorced Margie when she persistently suggested "starting a family." With each marriage and subsequent divorce her guilt feelings about her ability to be a good wife magnified. With the loss of her previous patterns of coping the third divorce precipitated this crisis.

After the third session Margie's depression and symptoms had lessened as she recognized the possibility that the failure of her marriages may not have been in her "inability to be a good wife" but in the disparity between what she wanted and expected from a marriage and what the men she had married wanted and expected.

Anticipatory planning

Exploration with Margie about her usual modes of social contact and her impulsive marriages (usually after only three or four weeks' courtship) assisted her in viewing her current divorce in more realistic terms. This was an important phase in anticipatory planning.

By the fourth week Margie had made significant changes in her patterns of living. She moved from the apartment she had previously shared with her husband to a small house near her mother. She also signed the papers to contest the divorce and found a new job.

Margie was granted the divorce and was apparently able to view her past experience as a traumatic but valuable learning experience.

In discussion and review with Margie of her future plans, she was cautious but realistic. She was enjoying her new job and new friends, going to movies and occasionally dinner with girlfriends. She stated that she was not accepting dates from men yet, "although I've been asked," and that if she married again, "it would not be in Las Vegas!"

Before termination Margie and the therapist reviewed and assessed the adjustments she had made in coping with the crisis, the insight she had gained into her own feelings, and her needs regarding future plans.

At termination Margie was reassured that she could obtain assistance in any future acute crisis that might occur.

Summation of the paradigm

Margie's inability to cope with a third divorce was precipitated by the lack of her usual situational supports, that is, her involvement and social contacts at work. This was also the first time Margie was forced into the role of an active participant in the divorce process, and she had no previous coping skills. Her inability to work due to illness further isolated her from her usual contacts, and she began to introspect about her previous divorces and saw herself as a failure as a woman. As her doubts increased, her feelings of guilt and failure magnified until she feared complete loss of emotional control.

The intervention was focused on encouraging Margie to bring her feelings of failure and guilt into the open. By direct questioning and reflecting the information back to Margie it became possible for her to view her current divorce and its effect on her in more realistic terms. She was given support by the therapist as she began to explore what she wanted and expected from marriage in the future.

DEATH AND THE GRIEF PROCESS
Theoretical concepts

To all who are living, death is certain. This universal phenomenon has ominous presence in that it is realistic and inescapable. Since every human being will at some time be subject to death, it seems that death is most significant. Much is unknown of the process of death, and human beings are noted for their fear of the unknown. It might be said that this is a basic fear, and throughout the ages man has sought self-preservation. Advances in medical science as well as allied areas support this contention.

The critical question is not the sham dichotomy of life and death but the way in which each person relates to the knowledge that death is certain. This fear may be the prototype of human anxiety. Throughout history, death has posed an external mystery that is the core of religious and philosophical systems of thought. Anxiety relates to the fact that man is powerless; he may postpone death, he may lessen its physical pain, he may rationalize it away or deny its very existence, but he cannot escape it and so the fight for self-preservation is inevitably lost.

The attitudes of the persons involved in the situation are basic to the process of dying. Concepts, philosophies, and attitudes about death evolve from centuries of conflicting ideas and thought.

Traditionally the attitude of a society toward death has been a function of its religious beliefs. Religion denies the finality of death and affirms the continuation of the human personality either in its psychophysical totality or as a soul. The medical and social sciences, by challenging these traditional beliefs, have indirectly caused alienation and a serious mental health problem.

Family reaction to the death of a member develops in stages varying in time. The death of a loved one must produce an active expression of feeling in the normal course of events. Omission of such a reaction is to be considered as much a variation from the normal as is an excess in time and intensity. Unmanifested grief will be found expressed in some way or another; each new loss can cause grief for the current loss as well as reactivate the grieving process of previous episodes.

Lindemann[9] states that following the loss there are three phases of mourning.

Phase I. Shock and disbelief. There is a focus on the original object with symptoms of somatic distress occurring in waves, lasting from twenty minutes to an hour at a time, a feeling of tightness in the throat, choking with shortness of breath, need for sighing, an empty feeling in the abdomen, and lack of muscular power. There is commonly a slight sense of unreality, a feeling of increased emotional distance from other people, and an intense preoccupation with the image of the deceased.

There is a strong preoccupation with feelings of guilt, and the bereaved searches the time before death for evidence of failure to do right by the lost one, accusing himself of negligence and exaggerating minor omissions.

Phase II. Developing awareness. Disorganization of personality occurs in this phase, accompanied by pain and despair because of the persistent and insatiable

[9]Lindemann, Erich: Symptomatology and management of acute grief, Am. J. Psychiatry **101:** 141-148, Sept. 1944.

nature of yearning for the lost object. There is weeping and a feeling of helplessness and possible identification with the deceased.

Phase III. Resolving the loss. Resolution of the loss completes the work of mourning. A reorganization takes place with emancipation from the image of the lost object, and new object relationships are formed.

Engel[10] states that the clearest evidence that mourning or grieving is successfully completed is the ability to remember *completely* and *realistically* the pleasures *and* disappointments of the lost relationship.

In this phase one must also consider pathological mourning, in which there is an inability to express overtly these urges to recover the lost object. When all reactions are repressed, they will influence behavior in a strange and distorted way; for example, a schizophrenic's reaction to the death of a significant individual may be laughter. There may be a delayed reaction or an excessive reaction; or the grief reaction may take the form of a straight agitated depression with accompanying tension, agitation, insomnia, feelings of worthlessness, bitter self-accusation, and obvious need for punishment. Individuals reacting in this way may be dangerously suicidal.

Proper management of grief reactions may prevent prolonged and serious alterations in an individual's social adjustment. The essential task is that of sharing and understanding the individual's grief work. Comfort alone does not provide adequate assistance. He has to accept the pain of the bereavement. He has to review his relationships with the deceased. He will have to express his sorrow and sense of loss. He must accept the destruction of a part of his personality before he can organize it afresh toward a new object or goal. Although they are unwelcome, such phases are a necessary part of life.[11]

The following case study concerns a retired widower who is threatened by a second loss before completing "grief work" from the recent death of his wife. Initial assessment of the crisis situation provided clues in the determination that he was probably in the last phase of mourning and became overwhelmed by the threat of losing another highly cathected object, his son. The goal of intervention was to assist Mr. P. in reentering his social world and in gaining an intellectual understanding of the grief process as it related to his symptoms.

Case study: Death and the grief process
Assessment of the individual and his problem

Mr. P., 67 years old and recently widowed, came for help to a crisis intervention center on the advice of his family physician because of severe depression and anxiety. He described his symptoms as loss of appetite, inability to concentrate, restlessness, insomnia, and loss of energy. These symptoms had been first manifested a month earlier, following the death of his wife. He thought that they had been

---

[10]Engel, George L.: Grief and grieving, Am. J. Nurs. **64:**93-98, Sept. 1964.
[11]Lindemann: Symptomatology and management of acute grief, pp. 141-148.

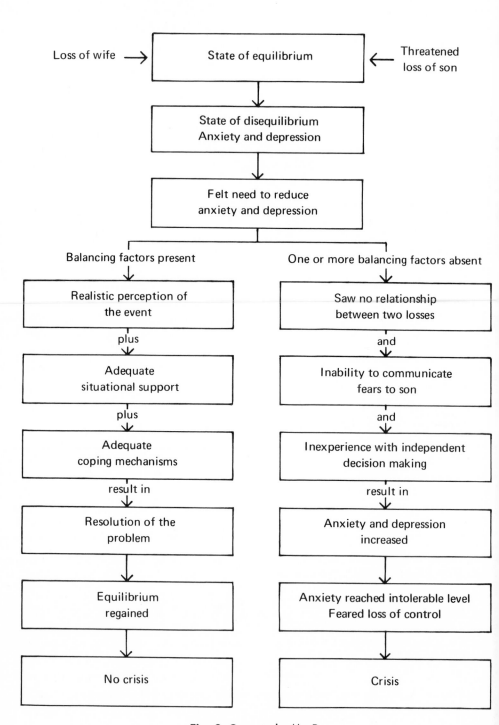

Fig. 8. Case study: Mr. P.

subsiding, but they suddenly increased to an intolerable level and he feared loss of emotional control. He denied any suicidal ideas, stating "I don't want to die, it's just that I've lost all interest in life and no longer care what happens to me."

During the initial visit, Mr. P. was, at first, unable to determine any specific event that might have caused the sudden and acute rise in his symptoms. His wife's death was not unexpected, and he had felt "well prepared" for a future life without her. He viewed himself as realistic in his attitudes and planning before she died and as having experienced a "normal amount of grief" afterward.

After a mandatory-age retirement when he was 65 years old, he had devoted most of his time in helping to care for his wife, a semi-invalid with severe coronary disease. "I think I was really glad when I retired, because I'd had so little time for myself in those last few years, working all day and then coming home and try-ing to catch up with things I had to do there." Having little time for social activities with his business friends, he had felt little sense of their loss when he left his job.

He had one son, married and living nearby. The son and his wife had close relationships with Mr. and Mrs. P., helping them out with their household activities and the care of Mrs. P. Mr. P. had made tentative plans to move into an apart-ment after his wife's death, feeling fully able to care for his own needs. However, just after she died his son and daughter-in-law brought up the idea of their moving into his home with him. It was a large home, much larger than their rented one, and they would pay him monthly amounts toward eventually buying it from him. He said that he was quite pleased with the idea, preferring to remain in his home but unable to justify to himself any reason for staying there alone. They had moved in two weeks ago, and he had felt an immediate lessening in his grief reaction to his wife's death.

A week ago his son had received an unexpected offer of a better job in another state. Mr. P. related that he felt very proud of the offer to his son, strongly urging him to accept it. The decision had to be made within the month. Since he had previously begun plans to live alone, he had not felt too concerned for himself if his son and daughter-in-law did decide to leave.

That same night he had suddenly awakened, feeling nauseous, tense, anxious, and very depressed, and sleep had become increasingly difficult as these symptoms had increased in the past few days. Although he no longer experienced nausea, there was a loss of appetite, insomnia, and a feeling of total exhaustion. He summed up his feelings by saying that he guessed "maybe I'm not as happy about my son leaving as I told him I was."

The therapist thought that Mr. P.'s recovery from the grief at the loss of his wife had evolved through the stage of shock and disbelief. He had anticipated her death realistically and had accepted it as inevitable. He had begun to overcome his feelings of guilt and sense of failure, as well as his persistent longing for a lost object (his wife). Mr. P. was probably in the last phase of mourning, that of emancipation from the image of the lost object and the initial formation of new object relationships. At this stage, before final resolution of his grief, he was un-expectedly threatened with loss of another highly cathected object, his son.

Planning of therapeutic intervention

Mr. P. had few social contacts because of his total involvement with the care of his wife during the past few years. His son and daughter-in-law had been providing situational support before and during his period of mourning, and this support was now in jeopardy. He had unrecognized ambivalence with regard to the job offer made to his son. Although intellectualizing plans to move into an apartment by himself, he lacked skills that would be necessary to repeople his social world. The anxiety generated by his unresolved grief and his ambivalence about his personal future was then compounded by the unexpected threat of a new loss.

When asked how he had coped with stress in the past, he said that he had always been able to keep busy caring for his wife and the housework. He had also been able to talk things over with his son. He now felt unable to talk to his son about his present feelings "for fear he might think he'd have to give up the job offer and stay here with me."

The goal of intervention was to help Mr. P. in gaining an intellectual understanding of his crisis in order to recognize the relationship between the threatened loss of his son and his present severe discomfort. His unrecognized ambivalence between his needs for independence as opposed to dependency would be explored.

Intervention

During the next two weeks it became possible for him to see the present crisis and its accompanying symptoms in relation to his reactions to the loss of his wife and the threatened loss of his son.

During Mrs. P.'s illness he had narrowed his own life style to conform to hers. In failing to acknowledge his lack of the interpersonal skills necessary to maintain a social life of his own, he justified his action as "what would be expected of any husband in a similar situation." Mrs. P. had been the dominant member of the marriage. Even when bedridden, she had guided the decision making that he thought was independent on his part. The additional support and assistance by his son and daughter-in-law only served to increase his dependency upon others for decision making.

At times during the past few years he had thoughts of "all the things we could have done if I'd retired when my wife had not been so ill." He had deflected these thoughts into overt sympathy for her rather than for himself and what he was missing. As her death became imminent and inevitable, his wife began to make plans with him for his future. She told him to sell the home and to move into an apartment, even selecting which furniture he should keep and which he should give away.

When she died, he was finally faced with the reality of his inability to cope with the changes. Crisis at this time was circumvented by the offer of his son to move into his home. He was able to continue in much the same life pattern that had previously existed for him, with the son and daughter-in-law assuming the leadership role. With their strong situational support the work of grief had not become overwhelming.

The sudden threat of their loss had precipitated the crisis. Unrecognized feelings of inadequacy and dependency had come into painful focus. He feared both the physical loss of his son and the loss of his son's love if the job were turned down "because he'd think I couldn't take care of myself if he left me here alone."

By the third session, through discussion and clarification with the therapist, Mr. P. was able to recognize his ambivalent feelings and relate them to his own needs for dependency. He saw the disparity between his concept of what he thought others expected of him and what he could actually achieve alone. His acceptance of this enabled him to reestablish meaningful communication with his son and to gain his support in making more realistic plans.

Anticipatory planning

Mr. P.'s exploration of his feelings related to his loss and subsequent grief helped him to gain an intellectual understanding of the process of working through the period of mourning. His recognition of his symptoms as part of the process helped to reduce his anxiety and enabled him to better perceive the reality of the situation and to utilize his existing coping skills. Realization was gained that he himself was withdrawing from available situational support because of his concept that his role was to be "an independent person." He was able to accept the fact that this might not be true and, as a result, felt better about communicating his fears to his son and enlisting his assistance in planning.

By the third week his son had made the decision to accept the position and move out of the state in another month. Through joint efforts they located an apartment-hotel for Mr. P., where he would have the independence to "come and go as I'd always planned for in my retirement." Since the hotel preferred its guests to be in the retirement-age group, there were programs established for the guests' interests and social needs.

Mr. P. moved into the hotel three weeks before his son left town. The period of transition was facilitated with minimal rise in his anxiety. There was a gradual removal of his son's situational support, which was being replaced by the support gained in new social contacts. Although he felt grief when his son and daughter-in-law left town, Mr. P. could recognize and relate his symptoms to the event and so was able to cope with them.

In discussion and review of his future plans Mr. P. was optimistic about his ability to live independently within the framework of his new environment. He was slowly entering new activities and making new friends, although he admitted "being a bit rusty about how to do it."

Before termination Mr. P. and the therapist reviewed the adjustments that he had made, as well as his new insights into his own feelings. He thought that the crisis situation, although being very painful to him at the time, had provided him with a "good idea of how to face up to things in the future." His future plans were also reviewed, and he was reassured by the therapist that he could always return for future help should the occasion arise.

Summation of the paradigm

Mr. P. had failed to recognize any relationship between his feelings of increased anxiety and the death of his wife. His inexperience with independent decision making made him inadequate to cope with the stressful event alone. Intervention with strong situational support by his son and daughter-in-law assisted him to begin to work through the grief process and averted a crisis.

The unexpected threat of his son's and daughter-in-law's departure and his inability to communicate his fears resulted in their loss to him as situational supports. These factors were compounded by uncompleted grief work and a failure to see any connection between his recurrence of severe anxiety and his reaction to a second loss.

In the assessment phase the therapist kept focus on the areas of stress to determine the adequacy of his past coping skills with bereavement. Intervention was directed toward assisting him to explore and ventilate his feeings of dependency. Anticipatory planning was directed toward providing him with situational supports when his son moved from town.

REFERENCES

Bernstein, Rose: Are we still stereotyping the unmarried mother? Social Work **5**:22-28, 1960.

Bowlby, John: Separation anxiety, Int. J. Psychoanal. **41**:89-113, 1960.

Brown, H. F., Burditt, Vera B., and Lidell, W. W.: The crisis of relocation. In Parad, H. J., editor: Crisis intervention, New York, 1965, Family Service Association of America, pp. 248-260.

Caplan, Gerald: An approach to community mental health, New York, 1961, Grune & Stratton, Inc.

Chown, Sheila M., editor: Human ageing, Baltimore, Md., 1972, Penguin Books Inc.

Claridge, Gordon: Drugs and human behavior, Middlesex, Eng., 1972, Pelican, Hazel Watson & Viney Ltd.

Croog, S. H., Levine, S., and Lurie, Z.: The heart patient and the recovery process, Soc. Sci. Med. **2**:111-164, 1968.

Glass, A. T.: Observations upon the epidemiology of mental illness in troops during warfare, Symposium on Preventive and Social Psychiatry, Washington, D. C., 1957, Walter Reed Army Institute of Research, U. S. Government Printing Office.

Greene, Bernard L.: Sequential marriage; repetition or change. In Rosenbaum, S., and Alger, I., editors: The marriage relationship, New York, 1968, Basic Books, Inc., Publishers, pp. 293-306.

Hellerstein, H., and Goldstone, E.: Rehabilitation of patients with heart disease, Postgrad. Med. **15**:265, 1954.

Hinkle, L. E., Jr.: Social factors and coronary heart disease, Soc. Sci. Med. **2**:107-110, 1968.

Hollender, M. H.: The psychology of medical practice, Philadelphia, 1958, W. B. Saunders Co.

King, S. H.: Perceptions of illness and medical practice, New York, 1962, Russell Sage Foundation.

Kubie, L. S., cited by Kaufman, J. G., and Becker, M.D.: Rehabilitation of the patient with myocardial infarction, Geriatrics **10**:355, 1955.

Laurie, Peter: Drugs; medical, psychological and social facts, ed. 2, 1971, Middlesex, Eng., Pelican, C. Nicholls & Co. Ltd.

Lee, P. R., and Bryner, S.: Introduction to a symposium on rehabilitation in cardiovascular disease, Am. J. Cardiol. **7**:315, 1961.

Linton, Ralph: Culture and mental disorders, Springfield, Ill., 1956, Charles C Thomas, Publisher, pp. 42-63.

McIver, J.: Psychiatric aspects of cardiovascular diseases in industry. In Warshaw, L. J., editor: The heart in industry, New York, 1960, Harper & Row, Publishers.

Milbauer, Barbara: Drug abuse and addiction, New York, 1970, The New American Library, Inc.

Moore, H. E.: Tornadoes over Texas; a study of Waco and San Angelo in disaster, Austin, Texas, 1958, University of Texas Press.

Parsons, F.: The social system, New York, 1951, The Free Press, Division of the Macmillan Co.

Rapoport, Rhona: Normal crises, family structure, and mental health, Family Process **2:**68-80, 1963.

Rehabilitation of patients with cardiovascular diseases, technical report series, Geneva, 1966, World Health Organization.

Reiser, M. F.: Emotional aspects of cardiac disease, Am. J. Psychiatry **107:**781, 1951.

Vernick, J.: The use of the life space interview on a medical ward, Social Casework **44:**465-469, 1963.

Zinberg, Norman E., and Robertson, John A.: Drugs and the public, New York, 1972, Simon and Schuster.

ADDITIONAL READINGS

Dahlstrom, Edmund, editor: The changing roles of men and women, Boston 1971, Beacon Press.

Lampe, Matthew: Drugs; information for crisis treatment, Beloit, Wis. 1972, Stash Press.

Shick, J. F. E., and Smith, D. E.: Analysis of the L. S. D. flashback, J. Psychedelic Drugs **5:**1-12, Sept. 1970.

Smart, R. G., and Bateman, K.: Unfavorable reaction to L. S. D., Can. Med. Assoc. J. **97:**1214-1221, 1967.

Wellisch, David K., and Gay, George R.: The walking wounded; emergency psychiatric intervention in a heroin addict population, Drug Forum **1:**137-144, Jan. 1972.

7 Maturational crises

An individual's life style is continually subject to change by the ongoing processes of maturational development, shifting situations within his environment, or a combination of both. Potential crisis areas occur during the periods of great social, physical, and psychological change experienced by all human beings in the normal growth process. These changes could occur during concomitant biological and social role transitions such as birth, puberty, young adulthood, marriage, illness or death of a family member, the climacteric, old age, and so forth.

Maturational crises have been described as normal processes of growth and development. They usually evolve over an extended period of time, such as the transition into adolescence, and they frequently require that the individual make many characterological changes. There may be an awareness of increased feelings of disequilibrium, but intellectual understanding of any correlation with normal developmental change may be inadequate.

The hazardous situations that occur in daily life may serve to compound normal maturational crises. When an individual requests help at these times, it is necessary to determine what part of the presenting symptomatology is due to transitional maturational stages and what, in turn, is due to a stressful event in his current social orbit.

The theoretical concepts used in this chapter are derived primarily from Erikson's (1950, 1959, 1963) psychosocial maturational tasks (trust, autonomy, initiative, industry, identity, intimacy, generativity, and integrity); Piaget's (1963) ontogenetic development of intellectual abilities (sensorimotor—birth to 2 years; preoperational thought—2 to 7 years; concrete operations—7 to 11 years; and formal operations—11 to 14 years); and Cameron's (1963) personality development, which is based on a synthesis of recent theories of general psychology and dynamic psychopathology.

For the sake of clarity the maturational crises discussed in this chapter will be presented in the more generally familiar phases: infancy and early childhood, preschool, prepuberty, adolescence, young adulthood, adulthood, late adulthood, and old age.

The case studies and paradigms presented here illustrate some common maturational crises. It must be emphasized that seldom are hazardous events and maturational crises this clearly defined.

INFANCY AND EARLY CHILDHOOD
Theoretical concepts

The first year of life is one of almost total helplessness and dependency. The infant must learn to trust the maternal figure and become able to allow her out of his sight without fear or rage. He must also be able to develop confidence in the sameness and continuity of his environment and to internalize it through his developing tactile, auditory, olfactory, and visual senses. Deprivation in any one or a combination of these senses could lead to maladaptive response patterns affecting his biopsychosocial development.

During this stage, the symbiotic relationship that develops between the infant and the maternal figure forms a foundation for the behavioral patterns of later personality development. This relationship goes beyond the symbiosis of mutual dependency for biological survival; in the psychosocial development of the infant it implies that the mother is willing and ready to assume responsibility for the infant, who in turn accepts her care passively without reciprocating.

During infancy the mouth is the primary organ of gratification and exploration; feeding becomes an important aspect of meeting needs. This is controlled by someone else, usually the mother, and her consistency in meeting her infant's needs for oral gratification is the beginning of his development of trust in his environment.

As a result of the varied experiences that he and his mother share, the infant develops confidence that his needs will be met. Through her own dependability, the mother structures these situations so that there is a basis for a mutual sense of confidence. For example, if the infant is fed regularly at times when he has come to expect a feeding, his sense of trust is encouraged. But, should the feedings become sporadic, he will become uncertain and anxious about his environment, and a sense of mistrust will begin to appear. His resulting fretful, anxious behavior may inspire further inadequate mothering. Another essential component of the healthy symbiotic relationship is the comfort brought by the mother; if discomfort is inflicted, any continued trust can be destroyed.

Environmental consistency and stimulation are important for cognitive and effective growth. The infant usually becomes aware of his mother as a person by 9 months; absence of *mothering* can provoke symptoms of insecurity by the age of 4 weeks such as crying and rocking, following by withdrawal, depression, and even death.

Piaget (1963) describes the infant's development of intelligent behavior in this stage as *sensorimotor*. During the first year the reflex patterns he was born with are repeated and strengthened with practice. As a newborn, he is capable of grasping, sucking, auditory and visual pursuit, and other stereotyped behavior patterns. These can be activated by nonspecific stimuli in the environment; after being activated a number of times the response becomes spontaneous without further external stimulation. For example, at birth the infant is able to suck at the breast; continued practice improves his coordination and facility until this ability becomes well adapted to the goal of taking nourishment.

These primary reflex actions become coordinated into new actions. For example, the hand accidentally coming in contact with the mouth and initiating sucking movements may lead to more coordinated actions and to thumbsucking as an established form of behavior. Later actions become oriented toward objects in the environment that stimulate his seeing and hearing, and intentional behavior emerges as he seeks to repeat these actions. He learns to begin meaningful actions in sequence and to explore new objects within his reach, thus developing goal-oriented activity. In this way physical activity patterns develop into mental activity patterns of response.

By the end of the first year the stage of purposeful behavior is reached, and exploration of further boundaries of the environment is begun. Motor actions have gradually become internalized as thought patterns. During this period the trend is toward a higher level of sensory experiences and related mental activities. By the end of the second year there is a functional understanding of play, imitation, causality, objects, space, and time. By the age of 2 years a child can truly imitate such behavior as eating, sleeping, washing himself, walking, and so on.

If the child does not develop the beginnings of trust, in later life there may be a sense of chronic mistrust, dependency, depressive trends, withdrawal, and shallow interpersonal relationships.

During the second year the child begins a struggle for autonomy. He shifts from dependency on others toward independent actions of his own. As his musculature matures, it is necessary for him to develop the ability of coordination such as "holding on" and "letting go." Since these are highly opposing patterns, conflict may occur; one example is the conflict arising over bowel and bladder control. A power struggle may develop between the child and his parents, since elimination is completely under his control, and approval or disapproval become strong influences because of his parents' attitudes toward eliminative habits. The child is expected to abandon his needs for self-gratification and substitute ones that meet the demands of his parents, representing the later demands of society.

Cognitive development in this stage includes the first symbolic substitutions, words and gross speech. The child begins to manipulate objects and will look for hidden items. He recognizes differences between "I" and "me," "mine" and "you" and "yours." He also begins to manipulate others by words such as "no," and the origins of concrete literal thinking are developed; this is the period of *preoperational thought* that continues to the age of 7 years (Piaget, 1963). One of its characteristics is egocentrism, in which the child is unable to take the viewpoint of another person; at the end of this period, egocentrism is replaced by social interaction. The child has now formed concepts in primitive images, thing to thing. He cannot cope intellectually with problems concerning time, causality, space, or other abstract concepts, although he understands what each is by itself in concrete situations. His perceptions dominate his judgments, and he operates on what can be seen directly.

The psychosocial task during this stage is to develop self-esteem through limited self-control. The achievement of bowel and bladder control within the prescribed cultural expectations allows also for self-control without loss of self-esteem.

This is an important time for establishing a ratio between love and hate, cooperation and willfulness, and freedom of self-expression and its suppression. Failure during this stage is manifested in childhood by feelings of shame and doubt, fear of exposure, and ritualized activity; in later adulthood the failure to achieve "autonomy" is seen in the individual who is a "compulsive character," with an irrational need for conformity and a concomitant irrational need for approval.

PRESCHOOL
Theoretical concepts

Erikson (1950, 1959, 1963) believes that in the preschool stage the child has the task of developing *initiative*. He will discover what kind of person he is going to be, he learns to move around freely and has an unlimited radius of goals, his language skills broaden, and he will ask many questions. His skill in using words is not matched by his skill in understanding them, and he is thus faced with the dangers of misinterpretation and misunderstanding. Language and locomotion allow him to expand his imagination over such a broad spectrum that he can easily frighten himself with dreams and thoughts.

The prerequisites for masculine and feminine initiative are developed. Infantile sexual curiosity and preoccupation with sexual matters arise. Oedipal wishes can occur as a result of increased imagination, and terrifying fantasies and a sense of guilt over these fantasies may develop.

Initiative becomes governed by a firmly established conscience. The child feels shame not only when he is found out but also when he fears being found out; guilt is felt for thoughts as well as deeds, and in this stage anxiety is controlled by play, by fantasy, and by pride in the attainment of new skills.

He is ready to learn quickly and to share and to work with others toward a given goal; he begins to identify with people other than his parents and will develop a feeling of equality of worth with others despite differences in functions and age.

At 4½ to 5 years of age the shift from infantile to juvenile body build is rapid, and the beginning of hand-eye coordination as well as an intellectual growth spurt occurs. The social base of gender role is firmly laid down by the end of the fifth year. If this stage is successfully accomplished, the child develops the fantasy of "I who can become"; but if the child is excessively guilt-ridden, his fantasy is "I who shouldn't dream of it." The desired self-concept at the end of this stage is "I have the worth to try even if I am small."

Failure or trauma at this time leads to confusion of psychosexual role, rigidity and guilt in interpersonal relations, and loss of initiative in the exploration of new skills.

PREPUBERTY
Theoretical concepts

Prepuberty years are characterized as the learning stage; that is, "I am what I learn."[1] The child wants to be shown how to do things both alone and with others; he develops a sense of industry in which he becomes dissatisfied if he does not have the feeling of being useful or a sense of his ability to make things and make them well, even perfectly. He now learns to win recognition by *producing things*. He feels pleasure when his attention and diligence produce a completed work.

There is a slow but steady growth as maturation of the central nervous system continues. In terms of psychosexual development there is reduced pressure in the exploration of sensuality and the gender role while other skills are developed and exploited.

The cognitive phase of development includes the mastery of skills in manipulating objects and the concepts of his culture. Thinking enters the period of *concrete operations* (Piaget, 1963), and the ability to solve concrete problems with this ability increases, so that toward the end of this period the child is able to abstract problems. The solution of real problems is accomplished with mental operations that the child was previously unable to perform. By puberty the child exhibits simple deductive reasoning ability and has learned the rules and the basic technology of his culture, thus reinforcing his sense of belonging in his environment.

Self-esteem is derived from the sense of adequacy and the beginning of "best" friendships and sharing with peers. This also marks the beginning of the individual's friendships and loves outside of his family, as he begins to learn the complexities, pleasures, and difficulties of adjusting himself and his drives, aggressive and erotic, to those of his peers. By learning and adjusting he begins to take his place as a member of their group and social life. In making this adjustment he seeks the company of his own sex and forms groups and secret societies. The gangs and groups, especially the boys, fight each other in games, baseball, and cops and robbers, working off much hostility and aggression in a socially approved manner.

Feelings of inadequacy and inferiority may begin if the child does not develop a sense of adequacy. Family life may not have prepared him for school, or the school itself may fail to help him in developing the necessary skills for competency. As a result, he may feel that he will never be good at anything he attempts.

---

[1]Erikson, Erik H.: Growth and crises of the healthy personality. In Identity and the life cycle, Psychological Issues, vol. 1, no. 1, monograph I, New York, 1959, International Universities Press, p. 82.

The following case study is of a 9-year-old boy whose maturational development had been delayed by physical illness and the actions of an overprotective mother. His biopsychosocial skills were inadequate to meet the competition required by his peer group and made him unable to gain their acceptance.

Case study: Prepuberty
Assessment of the individual and the problem

Michael F., a 9-year-old boy, was referred with his parents to a crisis intervention center by his school counselor. He had missed five and one-half weeks of school, the first week because of a cold and the rest of his absences because of headaches and vomiting in the morning as he was getting ready to leave for school.

Mrs. F. stated that Michael had always been a sickly child. He had a hernia repaired at 3 months of age and was also subject to colds and allergies. Only the week before she had taken Michael to a hospital for a thorough physical exam, which included an EEG, lumbar puncture, and blood tests. The doctor told her that there was nothing physically wrong with Michael and suggested that his illness was "probably psychosomatic"; it was he who had referred them to the therapist.

Michael was average in height and slightly overweight, his mannerisms were awkward and his coordination was poor, he was pale but looked healthy, and he seemed embarrassed by the whole situation. Michael was seen initially by the therapist without his parents present. His speech was hesitant, immature, and more like that of a 5-year-old. When asked why he was out of school, he said he "didn't know." He said he was an A and B student in school and that he disliked the recess period (during which the boys engaged in sports) because he was never picked for a team. He thought that he had no friends because of his dislike for sports and because the other boys said he "talked like a baby."

After seeing Michael alone the therapist talked to his parents to verify the information she had received from him and to assess their feelings about his problems and their ability to cope with them. Mrs. F. was a small, nervous, alert woman who had been in psychotherapy herself for the past few years. Her sister had died of nephritis a few months earlier, and she was concerned that Michael was exhibiting the same symptoms. Mr. F. was a rugged, handsome man, interested in sports and the business world. He said his relationship with Michael had been good until the present illness, but recently he had been unable to relate to Michael because of all the restrictions his wife had placed upon their activities.

Michael had a history of frequent illness and had become extremely dependent upon his mother, who encouraged this dependency. The school situation was forcing Michael to relate to his peer group, whose interests were in sports and cooperative activities; but Michael's dependency upon his mother left him unprepared to enter his peer group, and he had no coping mechanisms in his repertoire with which to handle his anxieties.

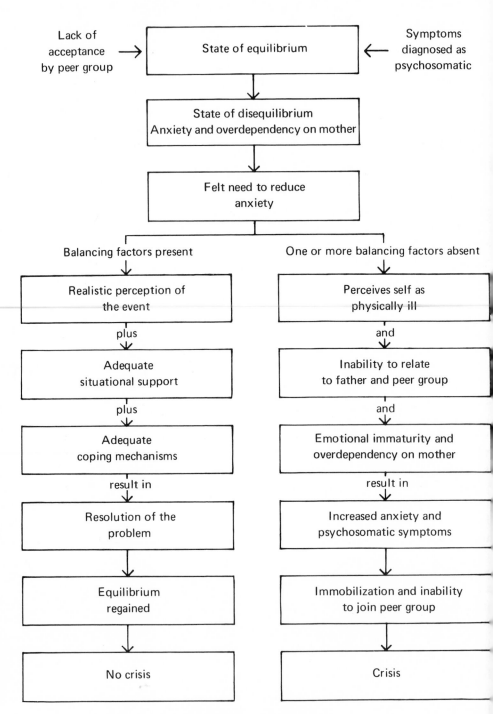

Fig. 9. Case study: Michael.

Planning of therapeutic intervention

It was thought that Michael's mother and father needed assistance in gaining a realistic, intellectual understanding of the situation. The mother's imagined fears of Michael's serious illness were based on a recent and traumatic experience with her sister. She received little situational support from her husband because he was impatient with her for giving in to Michael's attempts to avoid school and its athletic activities through his morning illnesses. Michael needed to explore his feelings of rejection by the boys at school and to express the fears instilled in him by his mother. Mr. F. needed to take a more active role in his relationship with Michael and to help his wife to allay her fears about Michael's imagined illnesses.

Intervention

Because Mrs. F. continued to imagine new illnesses for her son and to seek additional diagnostic procedures, the first goal of intervention determined by the therapist was to reassure her, by reinforcement of the doctor's statement, that there was nothing physically wrong with Michael. Another goal was to help her to realize that Michael's overdependency upon her had impaired his ability to function effectively in school and with those in his own age group. Mr. F. needed to become more actively involved with his son. Michael would require support to allow him to express his feelings of inadequacy about relations with his peer group and in dealing with school activities.

The therapist worked with Michael during the first part of each session, exploring his experiences at school during the previous week. The therapist would ask if Michael had attended school all week and ask for explanations of any absences. Michael's feelings about himself in relation to his peer group were dealt with at this time; the remainder of the hour was spent with his parents. Mrs. F. was continually reassured that Michael was physically well and could engage in activities normal for boys of his age. She was encouraged to retire into the background and to allow the father to take over some of the planning for Michael; Mr. F., in turn, was encouraged to insist that Michael attend school despite morning vomiting episodes. On those mornings when his father was unable to drive him to school, Michael was to ride his bike.

Mrs. F. agreed to this with reluctance, but was seen by the therapist as an effort by her to allow him more independence. Mr. F. tried to become more involved with Michael by taking him to his place of work during school vacation periods and letting the boy help him. These events helped Michael to gain self-confidence, and this new independence permitted him to interact more with his peers.

Anticipatory planning

Anticipatory planning revolved around showing the parents that their new behavior was a beginning step in allowing their son to be an independent individual, and the importance of continuing to make him feel that he had capabilities and that they had confidence in him was stressed. The parents were prepared for the next step for freedom because his need for independence would grow, and Mrs. F., particularly, needed to anticipate this so that she would be prepared to allow him more opportunity for growth and independence.

Mr. F. had stayed in the background because he believed that the major responsibility for child rearing belonged to the mother. He wished to be with his son more but had hesitated to overrule his wife when they differed regarding Michael's activities. It was pointed out to him that Michael's conception of masculine behavior would develop largely as a result of interaction with his father and that he should become more involved with Michael in the future.

Summation of the paradigm

Mrs. F.'s overprotection and fears of fatal illnesses served to reinforce Michael's feelings of inadequacy, and her anxiety about his physical well-being impelled her to curtail his activities and limit his involvement with his peer group, thus inducing and reinforcing feelings of inferiority.

When Michael's symptoms were diagnosed as psychosomatic, and Mrs. F. was still reluctant to give him independence, Michael became convinced that "mother was right" and that he was physically ill. As a result, his anxiety and resultant psychosomatic involvement increased, and he avoided school where participation in physical activities with his peers was necessary. His overdependence upon his mother and emotional immaturity alienated his father, and Michael was unable to turn to him for support; his symptoms increased, he was unable to attend school, and a crisis was precipitated.

Intervention focused on letting Michael explore his feelings of anxiety and inadequacy, and time was spent in working with his parents to help them understand how much he needed reassurance with regard to his adequacy and abilities. Mr. F. was encouraged to become more involved with Michael to counterbalance Mrs. F.'s overprotectiveness.

ADOLESCENCE
Theoretical concepts

The adolescent has a strong need to find and confirm his identity. There is rapid body growth equaling that of early childhood but compounded by the addition of physical-genital maturity. Faced with the physiological revolution within himself, the adolescent is also concerned with consolidating his social roles. He is preoccupied with the difference between what he appears to be in the eyes of others and what he feels himself to be; in searching for a new sense of continuity, some adolescents must refight crises left unresolved in previous years.

Changes that occur as secondary sex characteristics emerge, making the adolescent self-conscious and uncomfortable with himself and with his friends. Body image changes, and he constantly seeks validation that these physiological changes are "normal" because he feels different and is dissatisfied with how he thinks he looks. If sudden spurts of growth occur, he concludes he will be too tall; conversely, if growth does not occur as expected, he thinks he will be too short, or too thin, or too fat. In this period of fluctuation, half-child and half-adult, the adolescent reacts with childish rebellion one day and with adult maturity the next.

The adolescent is as unpredictable to himself as he is to parents and other adults. On the one hand he seeks freedom and rebels against authority, on the other he does not trust his own sense of emerging maturity and covertly seeks guidelines from adults. In his struggle for an identity he turns to his peers and adopts their mode of dress, mannerisms, vocabulary, and code of behavior, often to the distress of adult society. There is a desperate need to belong, to feel accepted, loved, and wanted.

This is the age for cliques and gangs. The "in group" can be extremely clannish and intolerant of those who do not belong. Banding together against the adult world, its members seek to internalize their identity, but because of different and often rebellious behavior they are frequently incorrectly labeled as "delinquent."

Having achieved a sense of security and acceptance from his peers, the adolescent begins to seek heterosexual involvement. This occurs first at group-oriented social events such as dances, parties, and football games. As comfort and confidence increase, the adolescent progresses to more meaningful and deeper emotional involvements in one-to-one heterosexual relationships. Because of conflict between sexual drives, desires, and the established norms of his society, this stage can be extremely stressful, and again he is faced with indecision and confusion.

Occupational identity also becomes a concern at this time. There are continual queries by parents and school authorities about career plans for the future. Uncertainties are compounded when a definite choice cannot be made because of an inability to fully identify with the adult world of work. Having only observed or participated in fragments of work situations, the adolescent finds it difficult to commit himself to the reality of full-time employment and its inherent responsibilities. It is easier and more realistic to state what is *not* wanted rather than what is wanted as a career.

Piaget (1963) refers to the cognitive development at this stage as *formal operations,* the period in which the capacity for abstract thinking and complex deductive reasoning becomes possible. At this time the goal is "independence," and in midadolescence acceptance of the idea that it is possible to love someone and at the same time to be angry with him is one problem that should be solved. If this stage is successfully negotiated, the individual develops a capacity for self-responsibility; failure may lead to a sense of inadequacy in controlling and competing.

Because of the number and wide variety of stimuli and rapid changes to which he is exposed, the adolescent is in a hazardous situation. A crisis situation may be compounded by the normal amount of flux characteristic of adolescent development (Cameron, 1963; Erikson, 1950, 1959, 1963; Piaget, 1963; Zachry, 1940).

The following case study illustrates some of the conflicts that adolescents face while trying to find their identity, to strive for independence, and to win acceptance from their peer group. It also points out the need for understanding and patience on the part of parents as their adolescents grow up.

Case study: Adolescence
Assessment of the individual and the problem

Mary V., a 14-year-old high school sophomore, was referred to a crisis intervention center with her parents by a school nurse. During the past few weeks she had shown signs of increased anxiety, cried easily, and had lost interest in school activities. That morning for no apparent reason she had suddenly left the classroom in tears. The teacher followed and found her crouched in a nearby utility closet, crying uncontrollably. Mary seemed unable to give a reason for her loss of control and was very anxious. When her mother came in response to a call from the school nurse, they agreed to follow her advice and seek family therapy.

During the first session the therapist saw Mary and her parents together in order to assess their interaction and communication patterns and to determine Mary's problems.

Mrs. V. was quiet and left most of the conversation up to her husband and Mary. When she attempted to add anything to what was being said, she was quickly silenced by Mr. V.'s hard, cold stare or by Mary exclaiming in an exasperated tone, "Oh, Mother!" Mr. V. spoke in a controlled, stilted manner, saying that he had no idea what was wrong with Mary, and Mrs. V. responded hesitantly that it must be something at school.

Mary was particularly well developed for her age, a fact that was apparent despite the rather shapeless shift she was wearing. She might have been very attractive if she had paid more attention to her posture and general appearance.

When questioned, Mary said that she had not been sleeping well for weeks, had no appetite, and could not concentrate on her schoolwork. She did not know why she felt this way, and her uncontrolled outburst of tears frightened and embarrassed her. She was also afraid of what she might do next, adding that her crying that morning was probably because she had not slept well for the past two nights. At first she tried to brush this off as final exam jitters.

She evaded answering repeated questions about sudden changes in her life in the past few days. When the therapist asked is she would be more comfortable talking alone, without her parents, she gave her father a quick glance and replied that she would. Mr. and Mrs. V. were asked if they objected to Mary talking to the therapist alone. Both agreed that it might be a good idea and went to the waiting room.

For a time Mary continued to respond evasively. It was obvious that she had strongly mixed feelings about how to relate to the male therapist: Should it be "man to woman" or "child to adult?" Throughout this and the following sessions she alternated between her child-adult roles. The therapist recognized the role ambivalence of adolescence and adjusted his role relationship, using whichever was most effective in focusing on the problem areas and making Mary more comfortable

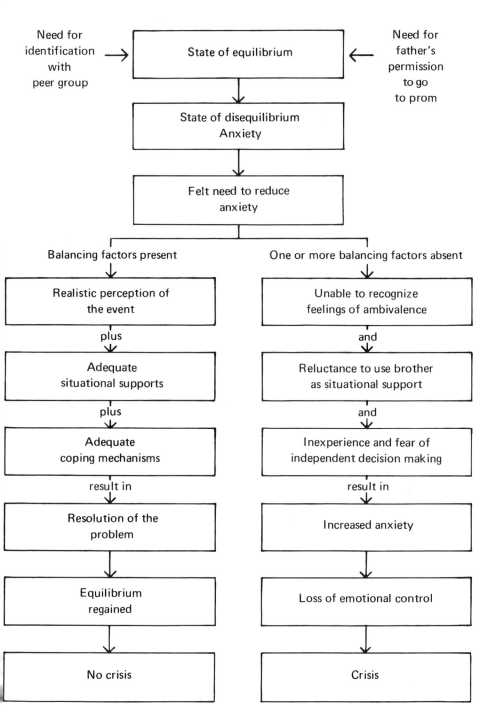

Fig. 10. Case study: Mary.

Mary eventually relaxed and began to talk freely about her relationship with her family, her activities at school, and some of the feelings that were troubling her. She said that she had two older brothers. The younger of the two, Kirk, was 16 years old and a senior in high school. She felt closer to him because "he understands and I can talk to him." Mary said that she had "as good a childhood" as the rest of her friends. However, she did think that her father kept a closer eye on her activities than did the parents of most of her friends. He still called her his "baby" and "my little girl" and lately had begun to place more restrictions on her friendships and activities than usual.

She admitted that during the past year she had gone through a sudden spurt of body growth and development. She was keenly aware of these differences in her appearance and sensed the changing attitudes of her father and her friends. She felt her father was worried about her growing "up and out so fast." He was the one who insisted that she wear the almost shapeless shifts. She said she knew "It wasn't really because I outgrow things so fast right now—he thinks I look too sexy for my age!"

About three weeks ago she had been invited to the junior-senior prom by a friend of her brother Kirk. She liked the boy and wanted to go but was not sure Kirk would approve, because he would be at the prom too. Another problem was getting her parents' permission to go and to buy the necessary formal clothes. She had looked at dresses and knew exactly the one she wanted but knew her father would not let her have it.

Mary was asked if she felt able to tell her parents these things that were bothering her if the therapist were present to give her support. She thought that she could if he would "sort of prepare them first" and explain how important it was for her to go dressed like the rest of her girlfriends. He suggested that Mary discuss the situation with Kirk to see how he felt about her going to the prom with his friend, and she agreed to do this before the next session. The therapist assured her that he would spend the first part of the next session with her parents to discuss and explore *their* feelings about this.

Planning of therapeutic intervention

It was thought that Mary needed support to assist her in convincing her parents that she be allowed to grow up. Mr. and Mrs. V. needed to gain an intellectual understanding of some of the problems that adolescent girls face as they search for an identity, seek independence, and feel the need to be like their peers. Mrs. V. would have to be encouraged to give support and guidance to Mary and help to resist Mr. V.'s attempts to keep Mary as the baby of the family.

Intervention

At the next session the therapist went to the waiting room to get Mr. and Mrs. V. and saw that Mary had brought her brother Kirk with her. She asked if he could come in with them at the last half of the session when the family would be together. The therapist agreed, realizing that Mary had brought additional support and that apparently Kirk had approved of her going to the prom.

The first part of the session was spent in discussing with the parents the general problems of most adolescents, as well as the reasons behind their often erratic and unusual behavior. Both parents seemed willing to accept this new knowledge, although Mr. V. said that he had not noticed any of this with the boys. Mrs. V. said, "No . . . but you treated them differently, you were glad they were becoming men." The therapist supported Mrs. V. and said that this was one of Mary's specific problems. He then repeated to the parents what Mary had said about the things that were bothering her. Both parents seemed slightly embarrassed, and Mr. V.'s voice and manner became quite angry as he tried to explain why he wanted to "protect" Mary: "She's so young, so innocent . . . someone may take advantage of her," and so on.

Discussion then focused on Mary's anxiety and the tension she was feeling because her father had made her feel different from her friends. Compromise between Mr. and Mrs. V. and Mary was explored when Mary and Kirk joined their parents in the last half of the session. Mary was more verbal with Kirk present to support her, and Kirk told his father, "You are too old fashioned, Mary's a good kid; you don't have to worry about her; you make her dress like a 10-year-old," and so on. Mr. V. was silent for a while and then said, "You may be right, Kirk, I don't know." He then asked him, "Do you think I should let her go to the prom?" Kirk answered, "Yes, Dad, I'll be there; she can even double with me and my girl." Her father agreed, adding that Mrs. V. should go with her to pick out a "fairly decent dress." Mary began to cry, and Mr. V. in great consternation asked, "What's wrong now?" She replied, "Daddy, I'm so happy, don't you know women cry when they are happy too!"

Anticipatory planning

The next few sessions were spent in supporting the family members in their changing attitudes toward each other. Anticipatory planning was directed toward establishing open communication between the parents and Mary to avoid another buildup of tensions and misunderstandings. Mary was encouraged to use Kirk as a situational support in the future, since he and his father were not in conflict.

The family was told that they could return for help with future crises if necessary and were assured that they had really accomplished a great deal toward mutual understanding.

Summation of the paradigm

Mary suffered acute symptoms of anxiety because she had to ask her father for permission to go to a dance. She wanted to be a member of her peer group but felt uncomfortable because she was not allowed to dress as they did. She wanted independence but was inexperienced and afraid to make a decision that would oppose her father. Because the situation involved possible conflict with her brother, she did not feel comfortable in talking with him about her problem.

Intervention was based on exploring areas of difficulty with the family and assisting them to recognize, understand, and support Mary's adolescent behavior, her bid for independence, and her need to become a member of her peer group.

YOUNG ADULTHOOD
Theoretical concepts

Young adulthood is the time in which childhood and youth come to an end and adulthood begins. It involves studying for a specific career or seeking employment, as well as sociability with the opposite sex and heterosexual behavior. According to Cameron (1963), socioeconomic developments make it difficult to determine the transition from adolescence to adulthood. Originally this was determined by the young adult maintaining an independent job, having the capacity for marrying, and forming a new family unit. The young unemployed tend to live at home with their families in a dependent relationship that has some of the characteristics of adolescence and some of the independence of adulthood. The young adult can no longer look forward confidently to gainful employment; without technical or professional education he may have to be satisfied with unskilled temporary jobs. The more time he spends in technological or professional training the longer he remains financially dependent on his family, and changes and uncertainties in modern socioeconomic situations may extend the period of dependence into the middle or late twenties. If the preceding stages of maturation have been successfully negotiated, the young adult will have confidence in himself and his ability for decision making and, as a result, will be able to establish and maintain a real intimacy with the opposite sex.

Adult society demands that he will not deviate from the established norm: the male is expected to remain in school if studying for a career or be consistent and productive in a job while maintaining an active social life. The female is also expected to be in school or working productively and establishing social contacts in order to meet and select her future mate.

There is an exploration and exploitation, or the denial of cultural and familial heritage, and a clarification of self-identity and the social role. The psychosexual task is one of differentiating self from family without complete withdrawal from the family. Cognitive development should be at the level of deductive and inductive logic, with expansion and exploration of cognitive capacities and the beginning of creativity.

Unsuccessful transition at this stage or lack of inner resources may lead to confusion when decisions are made regarding future goals. There is an inability to establish a true and mutual psychological intimacy with another person; there is also a tendency toward self-isolation and the maintenance of only highly stereotyped and formal interpersonal relationships, characterized by a lack of spontaneity, warmth, and an honest exchange of emotional involvement.

In the next case study a young adult is faced with the problem of making a choice between conforming to society's norms for choosing a vocation and marriage or remaining self-absorbed in his own immature interests.

Case study: Young adulthood

Assessment of the individual and the problem

Bob M., 18 years old, came for help at a crisis intervention center stating he was "feeling bad." When the therapist asked him to be more specific, he said he was not sleeping, was nervous, and things seemed unreal to him. When asked who referred him to the center, he replied a friend who had been there when he had been in trouble.

Bob was small in stature, slim, with longer than average black hair, neatly dressed in Levis, sport shirt, and motorcycle boots. During the initial session Bob appeared overtly nervous and depressed. He sometimes spoke in short, rapid bursts, usually after a period of silence but, more often, in a slow, hesitant manner. He would neither establish nor maintain eye contact with the therapist, continually looking down at the floor.

When asked about events occurring prior to the onset of his symptoms, Bob said that "during the past ten days so many things have happened it's difficult to remember what happened first." He began to recite events. After working on his car for six months "it blew up" the first time he drove it. This was also the first time he had been able to drive in six months because his driver's license had been revoked for speeding. This precipitated a quarrel with his girlfriend, Lauri, because he had promised to take her out when his driver's license was reinstated and his car was fixed. He had recently received a promotion to foreman at work, but he was ambivalent—pleased with the promotion although uncertain of his readiness to accept the responsibility of a permanent job. Last, his best friend, a member of the Hell's Angels, was out of town and he felt that he had no one with whom to talk about his problems.

Further exploration with Bob revealed that his usual pattern of coping with stress was to ride his motorcycle with his buddy "as fast and as far as we can go." They would stop someplace and "talk it out." He felt that this relieved his tension; things became clearer, and he could usually solve the problem.

Bob also expressed ambivalence in his relationship with Lauri. He loved her and wanted to marry her but was concerned because he thought that they had conflicting values; she was from a middle-class family with values that emphasized the importance of a steady job, conformity, and so forth, whereas he felt he belonged in the Hell's Angels' group and liked their philosophy, or as he stated it, "to be free, take what you want, don't work." He was afraid that marriage to Lauri would inhibit his freedom and that to please her family he feared he would have to give up riding with Hell's Angels, working on his car, and his long hair.

Planning of therapeutic intervention

Because of the many problems presented it was necessary for the therapist to sift through extraneous data and concentrate on major areas of difficulty. She de-

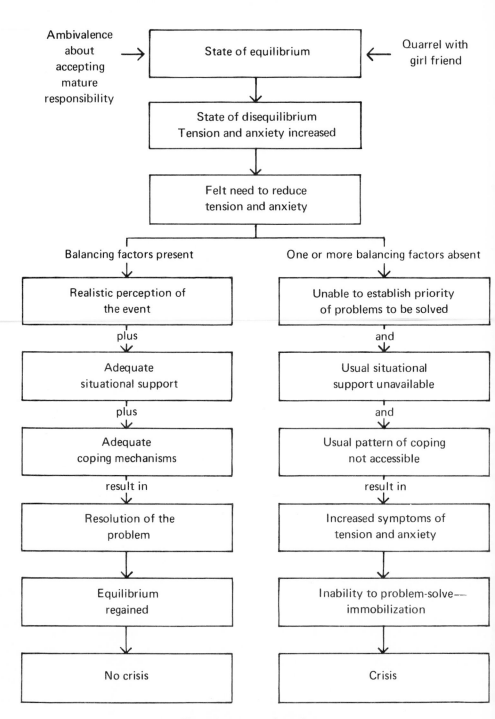

Fig. 11. Case study: Bob M.

cided, at this time, to assume the role of available situational support until other support could be found. This would give Bob the opportunity to use his prior successful coping device of "talking it out." As tension decreased, other support would be provided for his attempts to solve his problems.

Intervention

The goal of intervention was established by the therapist to assist Bob to recognize and cope with his feelings of ambivalence toward his job and Lauri and with the implications of making a choice. The areas of difficulty were determined to be a conflict of values and Bob's need to feel that he belonged to something or someone.

In the next two sessions, while the therapist acted as a situational support, Bob's symptoms diminished. He was able to discuss and explore his feelings about Lauri and his job; he also began discussing his fears of "giving up so much" if they married. Because Bob's relationship with Lauri appeared to be a major problem area, the therapist suggested that she be included in the sessions.

In the subsequent sessions, which Lauri did attend, they began discussing areas of mutual concern and conflict. Lauri said that she did not expect him to give up riding with Hell's Angels. "He can do it on weekends, and I'll go along." Bob became angry, saying that he did not want her along because she "was too nice for that crowd." He then admitted he was not certain he would continue with them anyway, *but* he wanted it understood that he could go riding with his friend occasionally if he wanted to. Bob added that if they were married, he might not need Hell's Angels because he would have her (his need to belong).

When Bob spoke of her parents' comments about his long hair, Lauri said that she liked his hair and that he was marrying her not her family.

She insisted, however, that Bob spent too much time working on his car and not enough with her. Bob replied that the car was his hobby and said that he probably spent less time on his hobby than her father did on his golf.

In the concluding sessions Bob apparently resolved his conflicts and stated firmly that he thought he would be gaining more than he might lose if he married Lauri and kept his job. At the last session they made tentative plans to be married.

Anticipatory planning

The most important phase in anticipatory planning occurred when Bob agreed that Lauri be included in the therapy sessions. The necessity of choosing between present modes of behavior and gratifications and future expectations in his life led Bob to weigh the consequences involved. His decision to include Lauri in future planning indicated an orientation toward reality. In certain phases of life it is necessary to give up certain pleasures of youth that appear to be consistent with freedom. An orientation toward the future, where maturity of decisions reflects not only an inner freedom but also a sense of self-fulfillment and a recognition of one's own strength, is consistent with a strong ego-identity.

Summation of the paradigm

Bob M. was forced to seek help because of increased symptoms of tension and anxiety. So many stressful events occurring in rapid succession had made it impossible for him to decide which problem should be solved first. His usual situational support, the buddy from Hell's Angels, was out of town, and his normal method of coping with stress was unavailable.

Ambivalent feelings about his job situation and his girlfriend Lauri increased his feelings of tension; he became immobile and unable to make decisions or to solve his problems.

Intervention focused on providing Bob with the situational support of the therapist, and Lauri was included as an active participant in the later sessions. When Bob was encouraged to ventilate his feelings, his anxiety decreased and he was able to perceive relationships between the stressful events and his crisis situation more realistically. Previous successful coping skills were reintroduced and proved adequate in assisting him to solve his problem. Major focus of the last sessions was anticipatory planning to help him cope with future areas of stress as he made the transition to increased maturity.

ADULTHOOD

Theoretical concepts

Adulthood is the usual period in life when the responsibilities of parenthood are assumed, involving the abilities of a man and woman to accept the strengths and weaknesses of one another and to combine their energies toward mutual goals. It is a crucial time for reconciliation with practical reality.

Maturity is always relative and is usually considered to develop in adulthood. Many adults who marry and have children never do achieve psychological maturity, whereas others who choose not to marry may show a greater degree of mature responsibility than many of their married peers.

Adult normality, like maturity, is also relative. Normality requires that a person achieve and maintain a reasonably effective balance, both psychodynamically and interpersonally. The normal adult must be able to control and channel his emotional drives without losing his initiative and vigor. He should be able to cope with ordinary personal upheavals and the frustrations and disappointments in life with only temporary disequilibrium and be able to participate enthusiastically in adult work and adult play, as well as have the capacity to give and to experience adequate heterosexual gratifications in a stable relationship. He should be able to express a reasonable amount of aggression, anger, joy, and affection without undue effort or unnecessary guilt.

In actuality it is unreasonable to expect to find perfect normalcy in any adult. Absolute perfection of physique and physiology are rare rather than normal, and an adult with a perfect emotional equilibrium is equally as exceptional.

This case study concerns a young woman whose lack of psychosocial maturity created problems when she was faced with the responsibility of motherhood. Her husband's competence and pleasure in caring for their baby increased her feelings of inadequacy and rejection.

Case study: Adulthood
Assessment of the individual and the problem

Myra and John, a young married couple, were referred by Myra's obstetrician to a crisis intervention center because of her symptoms of depression. Myra said she was experiencing difficulty in sleeping, was constantly tired, and would begin to cry for no apparent reason.

Myra was an attractive but fragile blonde of 22 years whose looks and manners gave her the appearance of a 16-year-old. John, 28 years old, had a calm and mature demeanor. They had been married a year and a half and were the parents of a 3-month-old son, John, Jr.

John was an engineer with a large corporation. Myra had been a liberal arts major when they met and married. John was the oldest of four children and was from a stable family of modest circumstances; Myra, on the other hand, was an only child who had been indulged by wealthy parents.

When questioned by the therapist specifically about the onset of her symptoms, Myra stated that they had really begun after the baby was born, with crying spells and repeated assertions that she "wasn't a good mother" and that taking care of the baby made her nervous. She said she felt inadequate and that even John was better with the baby than she. John attempted to reassure her by telling her she was an excellent mother and that he realized she was nervous about caring for the baby. He suggested that he get someone to help her. Myra said she did not want anyone, because it was her baby, and she could not understand why she felt as she did.

When questioned about her pregnancy and the birth of the child, she said there had been no complications and had added hesitantly that it had not been a planned pregnancy. When asked to explain further, she replied that she and John had decided to wait until they had been married about three years before starting a family. She went on to explain that she did not think she and John had enough time to enjoy their life together before the baby was born.

After she had recovered from the shock of knowing that she was pregnant, she became really thrilled at the thought of having a baby and enjoyed her pregnancy and shopping for the nursery. Toward the end of her pregnancy she had difficulty sleeping and was troubled by nightmares. She began to feel uncertain of her ability to be a good mother and was frightened because she had not been around babies before.

When she and John brought the baby home, they engaged a nurse for two weeks to take care of the child and to teach Myra baby care. She thought that basically she knew how, but it upset her if the baby did not stop crying when she picked him up. When he was at home, John usually took care of the baby, and his competency made her feel more inadequate. The precipitating event was thought to have occurred the week before when John had arrived home from work to find

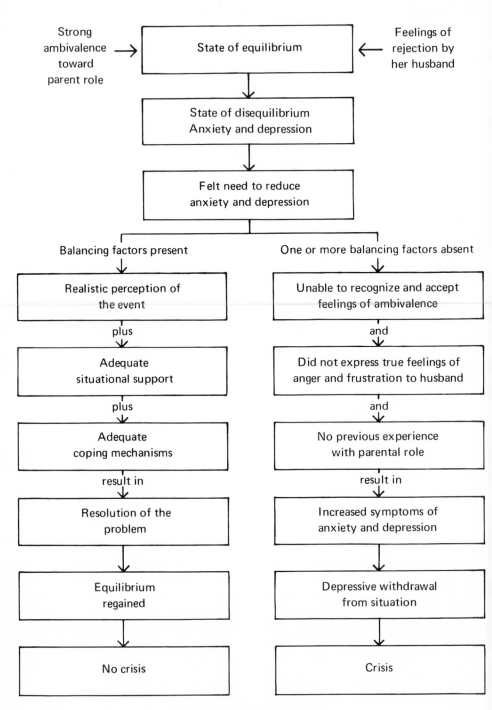

Fig. 12. Case study: Myra.

Myra walking the floor with the baby, who was crying loudly. Myra told him she had taken the baby to the pediatrician for an immunization shot that morning. After they returned home he had become irritable, crying continuously, and repeatedly refusing his bottle. When Myra said she did not know what to do, John told her the baby felt feverish. After they took the baby's temperature and discovered that it was 102° F., John called the pediatrician, who recommended a medication to reduce the temperature and discomfort; John got the medication and gave it to the baby; he also gave the baby his bottle. The baby went to sleep, but Myra went to their bedroom crying and upset.

Planning of therapeutic intervention

Myra's mixed feelings toward the baby would be explored in addition to her feelings of inadequacy in caring for him. She apparently resented the responsibility of the parental role, which she was not ready to assume. Unable to express her hostility and feelings of rejection toward the baby, she turned them inward on herself, with the resulting overt symptoms of depression. Bringing these feelings into the open would be a necessary goal. Myra also needed reassurance that her feelings of inadequacy were normal because of her lack of contact and experience with infants and also because most new parents felt this same inadequacy in varying degrees. John obviously was comfortable and knowledgeable in the situation as a result of his experience with a younger brother and sisters; he should be utilized as a strong situational support.

Intervention

The therapist, believing that a mild antidepressant would help to relieve Myra's symptoms, arranged a medical consultation. It was not thought that she was a threat to herself or to others, and intervention was instituted.

Myra's mention in the initial session that she and John had not had enough time to enjoy each other before the baby was born was considered to be an initial reference to Myra's negative feelings regarding her pregnancy and the baby. In subsequent sessions, using direct questioning and reflection of verbal and nonverbal clues, Myra was able to express some of her feelings about their life as a family with a baby in contrast to her feelings when there had been just herself and John.

Their previous life pattern revealed much social activity prior to the birth of the baby and almost none afterward. Myra said that although this had not really bothered her too much at first, recently she had felt as if the walls were closing in on her. John appeared surprised to hear this and asked why she had not mentioned it to him. Myra replied with some anger that it apparently did not seem to bother him, because it was obvious that he enjoyed playing with the baby after he came home from work. The possibility of reinstating some manner of social life for Myra and John was considered to be essential at this point. John told her that his mother would enjoy the chance to babysit with her new grandson and that he and Myra should plan some evenings out alone or with friends. Myra brightened considerably at this and seemed pleased at John's concern.

The therapist also explored their feelings about the responsibilities of parenthood and Myra's feelings of inadequacy in caring for the baby. Myra could communicate to John and the therapist her feelings that the baby received more of John's attention than she and that she resented "playing second fiddle." John explained that he had originally assumed care of the baby so that she could get some rest and that he enjoyed being with her more than the baby. He told her that he loved her and that she would always come first with him.

Myra was eventually able to see that she was being childish in resenting the baby and was competing for John's attention; as her social life expanded, her negative feelings toward the baby lessened and she said she was feeling more comfortable in caring for him. After the fourth session the medication was discontinued, and Myra's symptoms continued to decrease.

Anticipatory planning

Because of John's maturity it was thought important that he be aware of the possibility that Myra could occasionally have a recurrence of feelings of rejection. If the original symptoms returned, he would recognize them by the pattern they would take and would be able to intercede by exploring what was happening, discussing this openly with Myra. When the progress and adjustments they had made in learning to cope with the situation were reviewed with them, both expressed satisfaction with the changes that had occurred. They were told that they could return for further help if another crisis situation developed.

Summation of the paradigm

Myra was an only child and rarely had to accept responsibility for others prior to her marriage. Because she had planned to wait three years before having a child she experienced strong mixed feelings about the responsibilities of motherhood before that time and felt unprepared. Her husband's adequacy in caring for the baby when she failed reinforced her mixed feelings. Loss of the social life shared with her husband, combined with the diversion of his attention from her to the baby, reinforced her strong feelings of rejection.

Because she was unable to recognize and accept her feelings of ambivalence and was also unable to tell her husband of her anger and frustration she turned them inward. Lack of previous experience in caring for infants made her unable to cope with the situation, increased her frustration and anger, and resulted in overt symptoms of depression and anxiety.

LATE ADULTHOOD
Theoretical concepts

Late adulthood is the final stage of development discussed in Erikson's (1950, 1959, 1963) theory of maturation. If an individual has successfully negotiated the preceding stages, he should be mature enough to accept responsibility for his life style without regrets.

To the average person reaching late adulthood, the age around 50 years implies that life patterns have been fairly well set and no longer are open to choices for change. Anxiety results if a man or woman has not demonstrated some capacity for success in either family or career roles. Symptoms of this are frequently noted in such forms as excessive use of alcohol, psychosomatic symptoms, feelings of persecution, depression, and so forth.[2]

Our culture seems unable to place any firm boundary lines on phases of the aging process. The general tendency is to view life as uphill from infancy and over the hill and decline after reaching the peak of middle years. With cultural emphasis on youthfulness it is not unusual for a person of 50 years to view his future with regret for things left unaccomplished. Hahn[3] refers to this stage as "heads against the ceiling," a time when "The realization strikes home that the probability for appreciable advancement is remote . . . The ceiling is encountered relatively early by some and at an amazingly late time by others, but for all of us the ladder eventually ends at a ceiling." He further describes this as a period when "Younger men and women are beginning to crowd into the competitive economic, political and social arenas."[4] With the rapid technological changes affecting businesses and professions, younger persons are often better prepared to supply the necessary knowledge and skills.

Family life changes as children grow up and become involved with school, careers, and marriage. For parents it is a time when specific tasks of parenthood are over, and they must return to the family unit of two, making reciprocal changes in role status in relation to their children and to the community. New values and goals must be developed in the marriage to replace those values no longer realistic in the present; failure to recognize this need can open the way to frustration and despair. The wife and mother now has freedom from parental responsibility, but if her entire life style was centered around the parental role, she may lack interests, skills, and abilities with which to make the role change.

Menopausal changes occur in women at this time. Usually around the age of 45 years there is a relatively rapid decrease in activity of the sexual glands occurring over a period of two to three years. Sometimes this is accompanied by a syndrome of psychophysiological symptoms such as hot flashes, dizziness, cold shivers, and anxiety attacks. According to English and Pearson,[5] it is thought that personality plays a larger part of the symptomatology than the cessation of glandular activity. Many women go through this phase without any stressful symptoms; others become panicky and afraid of a loss of sexual identity.

There appears to be no definite evidence that sexual gland activity in the male

---

[2]English, O. Spurgeon, and Pearson, Gerald H. J.: Emotional problems of living, New York, 1955, W. W. Norton & Co., p. 43.
[3]Hahn, Milton E.: Psychoevaluation; adaption, distribution, adjustment, New York, 1963, McGraw-Hill Book Co., pp. 92-93. Used with permission of McGraw-Hill Book Co.
[4]Ibid., p. 70.
[5]English and Pearson: Emotional problems of living, p. 43.

undergoes similar rapid decline and cessation; however, men can experience symptoms similar to those of women at the same age period. English and Pearson[6] consider these syndromes to be neuroses rather than a result of any changes in the sexual gland activity.

The unmarried individual with thoughts of eventual marriage and a family is now faced with the reality of advancing years. This is a particularly critical time for the woman. If her reliance for social status and emotional security has been strongly dependent upon physical attractiveness, she faces the inevitability of physical decline. Like the man, she can continue her career interests; but she, too, may be confronted with limitations for further career advancements.

The following case study concerns a 40-year-old wife and mother whose planned changes in her family role after the marriage of her daughter seem to be threatened by the onset of early menopause.

Case study: Late adulthood
Assessment of the individual and the problem

Mrs. C., a 40-year-old, youthful-appearing mother of three daughters (ages 17, 20, and 22 years) was referred to a crisis intervention center by her physician because of severe anxiety and depression, as evidenced by recent anorexia, weight loss, insomnia, crying spells, and preoccupation, which had begun after a visit to her physician three weeks earlier. At that time she had been told that she was entering early menopause. Her youngest daughter was to be married in a month; the two older ones were already married and living out of the state.

She described herself to the therapist as having always been socially active both in community affairs and in her husband's business and social life. Mr. C. was employed as senior salesman for a nationwide firm selling women's clothing. His work required frequent trips out of town and much business entertaining while at home. She seldom traveled with him (because of the children) but was deeply involved with planning and hostessing his in-town social engagements. She said that she enjoyed this and had always been confident of her ability to do it well. Part of her wife role was to wear the clothes of her husband's company as an unofficial model, and her husband had always expressed his pride in her attractiveness.

In recent weeks she had begun to feel inadequate in this role, and strong feelings of doubt regarding her ability had begun to plague her. At the same time she sensed that her husband was becoming indifferent to her efforts to keep herself and their home attractive to him. Her symptoms had overtly increased in the two days just past, until now she feared a complete loss of emotional control.

Mr. C. was two years older than she. He was socially adept, and her women friends frequently told her they thought he was "such a youthful, good-looking, and considerate person." She herself felt fortunate to have him for a husband. He was aggressive in business and could be sure of advancement. She said they had always

---

[6]Ibid., p. 43.

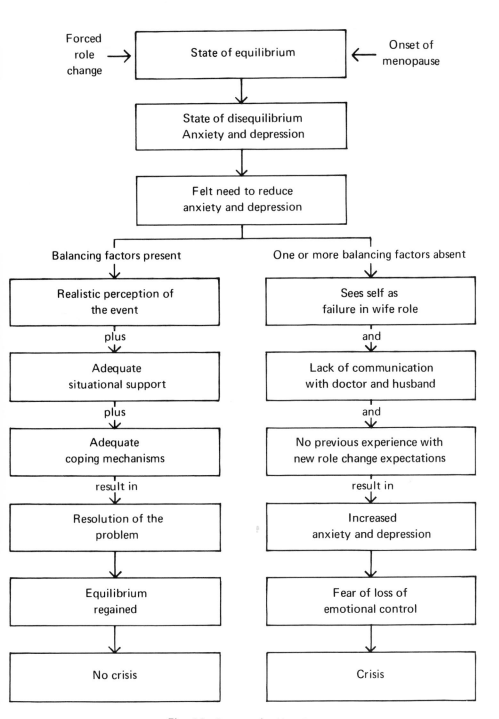

Fig. 13. Case study: Mrs. C.

been sexually compatible and shared interests and mutual esteem for one another.

When asked about what had occurred in the past two days to increase her symptoms, she said that her husband had come home two nights ago and found her disheveled and crying and not ready to go to a scheduled business dinner for the second time in a week. He angrily told her that he didn't know what to do and to "pull yourself together and find someone to help you because I've tried and I can't!" Then he left for the dinner alone. The next day he left town on a business trip after securing her promise to see a doctor.

Mrs. C. said that she had seen several doctors during the past few months because of various physical complaints. None had found any organic cause, but all had advised her to get more rest—one even told her to find a hobby. The last doctor, whom she saw three weeks ago, told her she was entering early menopause.

Mrs. C. had not told her husband of this, because she feared his reaction in view of her own negative feelings; her initial reaction had been disbelief. This was followed by fear of "change of life," as she had heard of so many unfortunate things that could happen to a woman during this time. In common with all women, she did not want to become old and unattractive and was angry that it could be happening to her so soon! She thought that she would no longer be an asset to her husband in his work because his clothes were not designed for middle-aged women.

Mrs. C. had looked forward to traveling with her husband after their youngest daughter's marriage. They had planned such a future together enthusiastically, and she felt proud to have contributed to his success but was now afraid that he would not need her anymore and that all her plans were ruined.

It was thought that the crisis-precipitating events were her expressed feelings of guilt and a fear of the loss of her feminine role. She was not seen as a suicidal risk or as a threat to others, although she was depressed and expressed feelings of worthlessness. She was highly anxious but could maintain control over her actions.

Planning of therapeutic intervention

Mrs. C. had withdrawn from her previous pattern of social and family activities. Her husband was frequently out of town, and the last of the daughters living at home had transferred many of her dependency needs to her fiancee. Mrs. C. in the past three months had felt physically ill and had narrowed her social activities to infrequent luncheons "when I felt up to it." Her peer group was in the 35- to 40-year age level and were all actively involved in community affairs, family activities, and so on. Conversation with women friends still centered around problems of raising young children, and she believed that because her children were grown she no longer had much to offer.

Her goals for a role change from busy parenthood to active participation with her husband in his business-social world were threatened, and she had no coping experiences in this particular situation. Previous methods of coping with stress were discussed. She related that she had always kept busy with their children and either forgot the problems or talked them out with close friends or her husband. She could not recall a close woman friend who had reached the menopausal stage and with whom she could discuss her feelings, and she was too fearful of the reaction she imagined her husband would have to discuss it with him. Her inability to communicate her feelings and the loss of busy work with her children eliminated any situational supports in her home environment, obviating the use of previously successful coping mechanisms.

Intervention

The goal of intervention was established by the therapist to assist Mrs. C. to an intellectual understanding of her crisis. It was obvious to the therapist that she had little knowledge of the physiological and psychological changes that occur in menopause. There was no insight to her feelings of guilt and fear of the threatening loss of her feminine role. Unrecognized feelings about her relationship with her husband would be explored.

During the next five weeks, through the use of direct questioning and reflection of verbal and nonverbal clues with Mrs. C., it became possible for her to relate the present crisis and its effect to past separations from her husband (business trips) and her previous successful coping mechanisms.

Mrs. C. had married when she was 17 years old. She described herself as having been attractive and popular in school, busy at all sorts of school activities. Mr. C. had been what everyone considered quite a catch. He came from a prosperous family, had been a high school football captain and class president, and was sought after by many of her girlfriends. At the time of their marriage he was a freshman in college.

She always had a high regard for her physical attractiveness and her ability to fulfill the social role Mr. C. expected of her. Throughout the years when he traveled alone, she felt left out of a part of his life and had looked forward with great expectations to being able to be with him all of the time. Knowing that his business brought him in frequent contact with attractive women buyers and models, she regarded her own physical attractiveness as a prime requirement to "meet the competition." With Mr. C.'s frequent trips away from home she had magnified her role in the husband-wife relationship to be more on the physical-social level than in the shared role of parental responsibilities.

Anticipatory planning

Mrs. C. never questioned her doctor after he informed her of his diagnosis of early onset of menopause, and obviously her knowledge was inadequate and based almost entirely on hearsay and myth rather than on fact. The physiological basis of the process of aging was discussed, and much of her fear was allayed. This was an important phase of anticipatory planning.

She was given situational support in which to talk out her feelings of insecurity in her marriage and to view it in more realistic terms. Relationships between the precipitating events and the crisis symptoms were explored.

By the third week Mrs. C. had made significant progress toward reestablishing her coping skills. She no longer feared "getting old overnight" and was able to tell her husband that she was entering early menopause.

His response was, "What the hell! Is that why you have been acting so peculiar lately? You might have told me; the way you've been carrying on anyone would have thought you had just been told you had six months to live!" Although her first impulse was to interpret this as evidence of his indifference to her as a woman, she later saw it as positive proof of her own unrealistic fears. She returned to her medical doctor as advised for continuing care and planning for any physical problems that might arise in the future.

By the fifth week she expressed confidence in her ability to meet the goals that she and her husband had set for their future. Their daughter had married, and Mrs. C. was ready to leave town with her husband on a business trip. Before termination the adjustments she had made in coping with the crisis were reviewed and discussed with her.

Summation of the paradigm

Mrs. C. had been unable to cope with the combined stresses of early menopausal symptoms and the need to change her family role. She avoided communicating her fears to anyone who might have given her situational support for fear they would confirm her own negative reactions. Increasing feelings of inadequacy, resulting in anxiety and depression, led to a crisis level of disequilibrium.

Initial intervention focused on the exploration of Mrs. C.'s knowledge of the physical and psychological changes that could occur in menopause. As she was encouraged to explore and ventilate her feelings about her relationship with her husband, her perception of the stressful situation became more realistic and her coping skills were reintroduced successfully.

OLD AGE
Theoretical concepts

Erikson's formulation of the stages of man's development stops with late adulthood. Unfortunately, he has not extended his analysis to crisis stages encountered by the retrenching organism.

In man the aging process must not be viewed only in terms of chronological years but with regard for the complex interrelationships of biological, psychological, and sociological changes that occur during these years. There is no exact age of onset.

Generally, psychologists look upon aging as a period of decline. The pace of physical decline is highly individual, occurring throughout life, yet it is most commonly attributed to the period loosely called old age. "Old age with respect to what?" is a most significant question. It could be one of many things—organic, sensory, or structural changes—and the significance of each is not fully understood.

Personality changes have been substantially investigated, but problems of interpretation have arisen because studies have been directed toward the segmentalized personality traits rather than the total organization or adaptiveness. Individual studies have found the aged to be "more set" in problem solving and to be "more stable" in their habits and tendencies than are younger subjects.

Abnormal behavior in the aged is difficult to diagnose due to the increase of organic damage with longevity. These abnormal patterns of experience and behavior develop along new lines with age and raise questions as to the exact nature of endogenous psychosis and what part is played by reactive ill humor or somatically based psychosis. Abnormal mental attitudes may develop as reactions to loss of influence, destruction of or unfulfilled life goals, onset of human isolation, and threats to economic security.

Considerable research has been done in social attitudes and forces creating the role of the aged in our culture. Goffman's[7] denotative grouping of total institutions defines those for the aged as being established to care for people thought to be helpless and insecure—the blind, orphaned, indigent, and aged. In essence this might define the negative attitudes of our society for the aged.

Our culture values mutal independence of the aged and their married children. Feelings of obligation on the part of adult children to support and care for their aging parents have declined with the establishment of social insurances of medical and other community forces. An exaggerated premium is placed upon the physical and psychological attributes of youth. When a culture assigns a role to the individual, his acceptance and performance of it depend greatly upon his conception of the role as it relates to his own self-concept.

Sullivan[8] refers to the "self" as the reflected appraisal of others that comes into being as a dynamism to preserve the feelings of security. As new evaluations are reflected, the individual is obliged to reconcile these new concepts of self with those preexisting. Increasing conflictual appraisals may result in increased tension and anxiety, leading to a state tantamount to the acceptance of, or resignation to, old-age status.

As in the first years of adolescence, these later years of life are characterized by physical, emotional, and social crises. The onset of physical infirmities may require that the aged person turn to his milieu for a measure of care and security. The presence or absence of environmental resources, as well as the degree to which help from others is required for survival, becomes of prime importance. The elderly who are economically secure, alert, and outgoing may be able to rise above social attitudes and be in the position of continuing to influence the lives of others, whereas those who are not in this position may be forced to play the roles designated by society's attitudes. Reisman's[9] three ideal-typical outcomes of the aging

[7]Goffman, Erving: Asylums, New York, 1961, Doubleday & Co., Inc., p. 4.
[8]Sullivan, Harry S.: Conceptions of modern psychiatry, New York, 1953, W. W. Norton & Co., Inc., pp. 19-23.
[9]Reisman, David: Individualism reconsidered, New York, 1954, The Free Press, Division of The Macmillan Co., pp. 484-492.

process are as follows: (1) the autonomous people with creative resources who use them to advantage in old age, (2) those who are adjusted and remain so, and (3) those who are neither and so decay.

A study of centenarians by Dunbar and Dunbar, as quoted by Solomon,[10] found a high correlation between longevity and a particular type of ego structure, and most of the subjects had chosen independence from their children as a way of life. In many cases they contribute to the support of their dependents, many have an active sex life into the very late years, and few were found who retired to do nothing. They were not susceptible to feelings of uselessness and had maintained involvement in activities in which they took pride.

An apparent correlation between the degree of ego organization in early life and the degree maintained in the senescent years has been found. Those with strong ego organizations seem better able to withstand the increased stresses and conflicts of later years.

Fear of death is not unique to the aged; its proximity is undeniably closer to some. This is verified as groups of contemporaries become smaller due to attrition by death. The old *are* living longer. Various studies and observations have noted that feelings of anxiety about death are most commonly coped with by the mechanism of denial, but it is not unusual to hear the very aged speak of "welcoming death" or saying that they "have lived a full life and have no fear of death." The social taboos that our culture places on frank discussion about death may lead to suppression of fear, to increased anxiety, and to resulting disequilibrium.

The aged are also faced with the fear of invalidism or chronic debilitating illness that might lead to dependency upon society for survival. This may lead to a regression to earlier childlike levels of ego organization as a means of adjusting. According to Slater,[11] the increased powerlessness and loss of authority status of the aged weakens the respect of youth. This may be followed by anger at the reversal in dependency roles, the ultimate destruction of the child role, and the anticipation of desertion by death. As a means of handling guilt that may arise due to ambivalence, young people project their feelings. It is the aged who become malevolent, isolated, and alienated and who are denied participation in society for all of the evils for which they are blamed.

Cumming and Henry (1961) have noted two critical events that take place during this period of life: retirement and the loss of a spouse. Both represent conclusions of central tasks of the adult life.

The widow finds herself with the loss of a highly cathected object, and other means must be found to redistribute the cathexis because she no longer has a social identity through her husband's occupational and economic status. She must develop a social identity of her own, based upon her own interests, economic

---

[10]Dunbar, F., and Dunbar F.: A study of centenarians. Quoted in Solomon, J. C.: A synthesis of human behavior, New York, 1954, Grune & Stratton, Inc., p. 237.
[11]Slater, Phillip: Cultural attitudes toward the aged, Geriatrics **18:**308-314, 1963.

status, and social skills as old social systems become closed and she is faced with finding and integrating into new ones.

Retirement is a highly critical time in a man's life. It is one thing if he has retired of his own volition and planning; it becomes more complex if it is mandatory. Losses include status identity based upon identification with his productive and functional role in society; he is also faced with loss of a peer group. Some men do not easily move to a role of pure sociability; this has belonged to their wives. Their focus of sociability has been directed toward their occupational peer groups, and loss of these groups through retirement leaves a void with few purely social skills to fill it.

Role reversal necessitated by a debilitating illness of a spouse is a fertile area for the development of a crisis. Rarely is either spouse prepared socially, psychologically, or physically to assume all of the responsibilities of such role change; the adjustments involved may be beyond the older individual's ability to cope and adapt.

It is evident that a continuation of maturational stages of development would be more difficult to define for the aged than for younger groups, since the processes of decline and growth occur concomitantly but not in equal balance. The process is highly individualized in all cases, and the variability of physiological, psychological, and sociological factors makes definite chronological relationships highly improbable.

When an elderly individual seeks help, his symptomatology requires particularly close scrutiny before an interpretation for intervention is undertaken. The therapist must first be aware of his own tendencies to stereotype the client's appearance and symptoms as a normal aging syndrome. Determining which of the crisis symptoms may be due to organicity is particularly important, since rapid onset of behavioral changes is not infrequently due to cerebrovascular or other organic changes associated with longevity. A professional review of the current medical history of the individual must be a recognized part of the initial assessment phase.

Too often the individual, because of organic changes, cannot gain an intellectual understanding of the crisis or recognize his present feelings. It may also be that those who directed him to the therapist are themselves in crisis; if this is true, the therapist may first have to resolve the feelings of the referrer that have been projected toward the aged individual who seems to be in need of help.

In the aging process there is need for the ego organization to withstand increasing biopsychosocial threats to its integrity, and unfortunately the individual's coping abilities may fail to adapt to meet the threats. The ability to accept new value systems and adapt to necessary changes in the achieved maturational development of earlier years without loss of achieved integrity may indeed be a developmental task for the aged.

REFERENCES

Cameron, Norman: Personality development and psychopathology, Boston, 1963, Houghton Mifflin Co.

Cumming, Elaine, and Henry, William E.: Growing old, New York, 1961, Basic Books, Inc., Publishers.

Erikson, Erik H.: Growth and crises of the healthy personality. In Senn, M. J. E., editor: Symposium on the healthy personality, New York, 1950, Josiah Macy, Jr., Foundation.

Erikson, Erik H.: Identity and the life cycle, Psychological Issues, vol. 1, no. 1, monograph I, New York, 1959, International Universities Press.

Erikson, Erik H.: Childhood and society, ed. 2, New York, 1963, W. W. Norton & Co.

Goldman, George D., and Milman, Donald S., editors: Modern woman; her psychology and sexuality, Springfield, Ill., 1969, Charles C Thomas, Publisher.

Piaget, J.: The child's conception of the world, Totowa, N. J., 1963, Littlefield, Adams & Co.

Zachry, Caroline B.: Emotion and conduct in adolescence, New York, 1940, Appleton-Century-Crofts.

ADDITIONAL READINGS

Bach, G. R., and Deutsch, R. M.: Pairing, New York, 1970, Avon Books.

Bach, G. R., and Wyden, P.: The intimate enemy, New York, 1968, Avon Books.

Chandler, H. H.: Family crisis intervention; point and counterpoint in the psychosocial revolution, J. Natl. Med. Assoc. **64:**211-216, May 1972.

Chown, Shelia M.: Human ageing, Baltimore, Md., 1972, Penguin Books, Inc.

Donner, Gail J.: Parenthood as a crisis, Perspect. Psychiatr. Care **10**(2):84-87, 1972.

Dow, Thomas E.: Family reaction to crisis, J. Marriage and Family, Aug. 1965, p. 363.

Foreman, N. J., and Zerwekh, Joyce V.: Drug crisis intervention, Am. J. Nurs. **71:**1736-1739, July 1971.

Friedman, Jacob H., and Bowes, Naomi: Experience of a geriatric crisis-intervention screening team, J. Psychiatr. Nurs. **9**(5):11-17, 1971.

Golan, N.: When is a client in crisis? Social Case Work **50:**389-394, July 1969.

Hinton, John: Dying, Baltimore, Md., 1971, Penguin Books, Inc.

Laing, R. D., and Esterson, A.: Sanity, madness and the family, Baltimore, Md., 1964, Penguin Books, Inc.

Langsley, D. G., and Kaplan, D.: The treatment of families in crisis, New York, 1968, Grune & Stratton, Inc.

Rubenstein, David: Rehospitalization versus family crisis intervention, Am. J. Psychiatry **129:**715-720, Dec. 1972.

Strickler, M., and La Sor, B.: The concept of loss in crisis intervention, Ment. Hyg. **54:**301-305, April 1970.

Thompson, Clara M.: On women, New York, 1971, The New American Library, Inc.

Williams, Florence: Intervention in maturational crises, Persp. Psychiatr. Care **9:**240-246, Nov.-Dec. 1971.

8 Levels of prevention and trends in crisis intervention

The concept of prevention is still relatively new when applied to psychiatric practices. Leaders in the public health field were among the first to recognize the need to include prevention and treatment of mental illness among their long-established community activities. Their early influence in this area can be recognized in the wording of the Community Mental Health Centers Act of 1963, which stated that its purpose was to provide "services for the prevention or diagnosis of mental illness, care or treatment of mentally ill patients, or rehabilitation of such persons." (U.S. House of Representatives, 1963, p. 19.)

At the *primary* level, prevention in mental health care is accomplished through anticipatory planning, counseling, and guidance. According to Van Antwerp (1970), this is not accomplished by just treating the ill as was done in the past. It will require intervening with both individuals and social systems *before* the disorders are manifested. Examples of these activities are programs in premarital counseling, child guidance, expectant parent classes, and programs with other groups or individuals who may be faced with major changes in life style or life space. At this level in prevention, vulnerable people, in need of more intensive intervention, may be identified. Other individuals may strengthen or even increase their levels of equilibrium.

Janis (1958) investigated the relationship between preoperative preparation and anxiety and postoperative adjustment. His findings suggested the need for staff to recognize that there may be precrisis periods in an individual's life during which anticipatory intervention, through guidance and support, can increase his abilities to cope and to successfully adapt to new life experiences.

The *secondary* level of prevention involves early case finding, diagnosis, and prompt treatment. Too often in the past this had been a less active level of prevention in community mental health care. While case finding usually took place in the community, it was more than likely coincidental with other community helping services. Diagnosis, prompt or otherwise, most often occurred in an institutional facility. It was primarily for this purpose that admission and diagnostic "holding" areas were created and staffed in large psychiatric institutions.

Within the past few decades, however, it has become increasingly apparent that institutional care can often do more harm than good for the individual with an acute psychosocial disturbance. Recognition of this fact has been a major force behind the current trend in developing innovative outpatient treatment programs as alternatives to inpatient care.

Prevention at the *tertiary* level includes halting further disability and providing rehabilitation toward restoration to a maximum level of wellness and functioning. According to Reiff (1966) and other writers, this should be a major goal of community mental health programs. At present, however, a great number of rehabilitation activities are still taking place in large institutions with minimal family and community involvement, rather than in the community with all of its practical realities.

All three levels of prevention are inherent and are practiced in crisis intervention. It is possible that this may be a major reason why the concepts and techniques of this method of treatment have been so widely accepted and integrated into a wide variety of community and institutional programs. As a result of this integration many institutions are also now extending their services into the areas of primary prevention.

New priorities are now being established, and roles are being redefined. New skills are being demanded, and many old traditional rituals are being questioned for their relevance. The patient is no longer willing to passively accept whatever treatment is meted out to him. Nor can his treatment be planned in isolation from him, his family, or others significant in his life. By necessity, treatment must become focused on helping him learn to cope and adjust to his life in the community—not to his life in the hospital. Those who, in the past, gave little more than lip service to the need to provide comprehensive planning and care for each patient are now being given both the opportunity and the mandate to put into practice what they formerly only preached.

According to Reissman (1970), a major concern confronting community mental health centers is no longer that of discerning just what services are appropriate to the needs of their potential clients. It is not even that of recruiting clients for the services provided. The centers are now being faced with the problem of obtaining an adequate supply of human resources to meet the demands for their services. Professionals and nonprofessionals alike are being recruited and trained to fill the gap between supply and demand for their services. This has led to the deprofessionalization of many mental health functions previously considered to be solely within the scope of the professional's skills. Role boundaries have undergone increasing diffusion as the needs of the individual client and his community become the determining factors in establishing the appropriateness of services.

It is not our purpose at this time to define the levels of educational preparation and experience of the various disciplines now practicing crisis intervention. Our intent is, however, to provide an overview of the current trends being reported in the utilization of available human resources.

PARAPROFESSIONALS

Increasing numbers of paraprofessionals are now being provided with additional education and training to function as consultants or "therapists" in mental health centers. Rusk (1972) reports an increased trend toward the use of paraprofessionals in functions once considered to be only within the domain of the highly skilled professional. Leaders in community mental health are keenly aware of the many dangers inherent in random, unplanned deprofessionalization of major mental health functions. Increasing concern is being voiced about the lack of definitive criteria established for the different levels of educational preparation and experience required of those who conduct the various "therapies."

As new roles and careers are being created, some are being formed within well-structured, formal educational and training programs. Others, however, have tended to evolve gradually and informally, often in response to specific needs of innovative programs.

Interest in developing more innovative uses for the relatively untrained nonprofessional worker has led to a wide variety of training programs being offered in community colleges around the country. Currently there are wide differences in admission criteria and program content. Wilson and associates (1971) have reviewed programs throughout the country. They report that much has been written on the recruitment, education, and placement of the paraprofessional workers, but little has been written on their acceptance by the consumers. They further suggest that the development of new careers in mental health may not be the complete answer to the highly complex problems raised by the shortage in skilled manpower.

A prototype of the model for new careers in mental health was established by Lincoln Hospital Mental Health Services in New York City. According to Collins (1971) in a report on this program, indigenous people were trained to serve as mental health aides in neighborhood service centers. Rather than functioning as an ancillary extension of the professional, these individuals served as liaison between the social and experiential gap separating the middle-class professionals and the lower-class clients.

Christmas and associates (1970) expressed concern that the inappropriate use of the paraprofessional in community programs could lead to perpetuating the past patterns of providing second-class services for the poor and minorities. This reflects a predominant theme of concern currently being expressed that the same patterns of care reported by Hollingshead and Redlich (1958) might be perpetuated in the new community programs.

All emphasize that the functions for which each paraprofessional staff member is utilized must not be determined by the scope of his preparation alone. They must also be determined by the amount of professional supervision and consultation that will be made available to him. The public is becoming increasingly sophisticated in its understanding of its human rights to equal care and treatment. It may not accept less much longer.

NON–MENTAL HEALTH PROFESSIONALS

Another resource for manpower being recruited into liaison activities with community programs is the non–mental health professionals. These are the professional individuals who serve as the official caretakers within their communities. Common to all is their traditional role of helping people who are in trouble. Included in this group are the medical professionals, teachers, lawyers, clergy, policemen, firemen, social and welfare workers, and so on. In the course of their daily work activities these highly skilled individuals can be found functioning in what could be called the front lines of preventive mental health care. They are frequently in contact with both individuals and groups who are in potential crisis situations because of a loss or the threat of a loss in their lives. Most often these professional community caretakers become the initial contact made by a person in crisis.

The contributions that this group can make to positive mental health education and practices have not gone unrecognized. Many new programs have been developed to include them as active participants on the treatment teams. How little or how much each can do is highly dependent upon the availability and willingness of the mental health professionals to provide them with training and consultation services.

NONPROFESSIONAL VOLUNTEERS

Nonprofessional volunteers are another source of manpower being recruited by mental health centers. Schindler-Rainman (1971) predicts that by 1975 approximately 70% of all work roles will be in people-helping fields. Individuals will have much more leisure time and will probably make themselves available as volunteers. Not only will they be utilized in the traditional volunteer roles as we know them today, but they will also seek training to develop skills to meet their human needs to be creative, to help others, to be recognized, to learn new skills, and to become meaningful members of the treatment teams.

Crisis hotlines, initially established by professionals and community leaders, rely heavily upon the nonprofessional volunteer for their 24-hour–day, 7-day–week services. According to Clark and Jaffe (1972), these hotlines seem to have originated in both the traditional and counterculture models of crisis intervention. Nonprofessionals were carefully selected, intensively trained, and closely supervised in these original psychiatric emergency centers.

Torop and Torop (1972), in their report on the use of volunteers in a crisis hotline program, call attention to the potential dangers for clients when unskilled volunteers are not provided with consistent and skillful professional supervision.

In particular they point out the need to recognize and intervene when a volunteer may be responding to his own personal intuition and bias.

Later developments in crisis intervention history were the organization of free clinics and similar community help centers. These are predominantly staffed by volunteers from the counterculture communities to whom they provide services.

TEAM APPROACH TO CRISIS

A recent development has been the increasing use of the team approach to crisis intervention. Crisis team members are selected on the basis of their expertise to meet the specific needs of each patient in crisis. Members will vary with the structure and requirements of the individual mental health centers, as well as with the geographic and socioeconomic needs of the community. The unique skills of each member are utilized from the time of initial contact until the crisis is resolved and follow-up support is no longer felt to be necessary.

Team membership is open ended, expanding and contracting within highly flexible boundaries. Leadership of each team depends upon who has the skills and expertise most appropriate to help the individual resolve his crisis. This is not to say, however, that ultimate professional responsibility is removed from the physician. Rather, there is a greater scope in delegation of authority to make decisions in treatment planning.

Informal and, at times, unrecognized members of the community mental health team are the nonprofessional community caretakers. These individuals in the course of their usual daily activities have many contacts with fellow members of the community or are sought out for help and advice. They act as a source of information and are an integral part of the communication channels within the social systems of the community. In their formal roles, such as cab drivers, bartenders, grocers, barbers, beauticians, and neighbors, they provide a sympathetic ear and situational support to those in trouble and looking for help. If informed and aware of the purpose and services provided by the center, they can be a reliable and direct referral source for those in need of crisis intervention.

The non–mental health professional caretaker's function is a more formal role relationship with members of the community. These caretakers receive their communications within the system from a nonprofessional caretaker or directly from the individual who needs help. They could be incorporated into the community mental health team as consultants or as persons who make direct referrals to the center for treatment.

Selected nonprofessional volunteers could be used in liaison within the community as interpreters with foreign language population groups and as sources of referral. With appropriate training in crisis-intervention techniques they could be utilized as "therapists" under the supervision of mental health professionals at some centers.

Paraprofessionals function as members of the team in accord with their basic training and educational preparation. In their roles at the center they could focus on initial assessments and observations of behavioral changes in the clients. If a client were retained for 24 to 72 hours on a crisis ward, members of this group could be prepared to participate in various adjunctive therapies under professional guidance and supervision. Their realm of functioning would be within the immediate environs of the center.

The mental health professionals could function on the crisis team much as they function on any mental health team. The psychiatrist, psychologist, psychiatric nurse, and psychiatric social worker could conduct individual, family, or group therapy as needed by the clients. The diversity of local demands and problems underscores ability and accomplishment of individual team members more than professional background alone. Generalization, frequently required on the part of the staff, may be one factor accounting for the less strict division of roles and responsibilities among the professional in a community mental health center.

The administrator's task would be to create a climate in which each team member is free enough and challenged enough to actively participate in the care needed by the clients seeking help to resolve their crises.

TRENDS IN RESEARCH

Within the relatively brief span of time since its development as a recognized treatment modality, the concepts and techniques of crisis intervention have become widely accepted in community programs both in the United States and in other countries. The lack of parallel growth in research activities in this field has, however, led many to question whether it will maintain a permanent place as a recognized method of treatment.

Subjective evaluations have predominated in current literature. Minimal empirical research has been reported. Problems in formulating comparative studies, control groups, and so forth are increasing as programs become more and more innovative in their efforts to meet the needs of their sponsoring organizations and the communities they serve.

One of the problems in evaluation of these programs is inherent in the concept of crisis itself. It is a concept of such global proportions that it can only be operationalized for research purposes by breaking it down into selected components. For example, since Seyle's work in the late 1940's, research into physiological stress has progressed continuously. The same precise work has not yet been accomplished in the study of psychological stress, leaving much confusion in trying to distinguish between the two. Introduction of the concept of crisis has only compounded this confusion.

There are few words so subjectively perceived as *crisis*. It has become widely used in the English language, and indiscriminate usage has caused it to lose much of its former meaning as a descriptive term. As a result there is frequently misunderstanding by many when they hear or read of crisis intervention as a technique being used in mental health programs. The word comes originally from the Greek word "krisis," which means "to separate." In medicine it usually refers to that change in disease which indicates whether the result is to be recovery or death. In international relations a crisis most often refers to an event or a conflict, the outcome determining war or peace. Its connotation is that of a decisive moment, a turning point. Its specific meaning in crisis intervention is derived from Caplan's (1964) definition.

Without first achieving empirical definitions to distinguish between physiological stress and psychological stress, research is now faced with a need to distinguish the *latter* from crisis. Rapoport (1962) has attempted to make this differentiation. She perceives stress as having pathogenic potential, and crisis as having a growth-promoting potential.

Caplan (1964) makes a temporal distinction between crisis and stress. He sees crisis characterized by a short time period, while stress need not be. Despite some efforts in this direction, Eastman and associates (1970) suggest that the general trend seems to be one of avoiding the issue and using the terms interchangeably. They further suggest that there must be a clear description of a crisis syndrome in order to establish criteria for noncrisis control groups in research.

Another problem in program evaluations is the need to have empirical categorizations of both the symptomatology of crisis and of the various contributing factors. Caplan (1964), Tyhurst (1957), Sifneos (1960), and Golan (1969) have described crisis syndromes, suggesting that there *are* definitive, characteristic stages in the development of a crisis.

Despite these and other extensive efforts to reliably define and categorize crisis as opposed to noncrisis, the question remains whether these are more than descriptive conveniences. There is still the recognized need to identify reliable criteria in order to assess the appropriateness of crisis intervention.

For these reasons alone the question of who can best do crisis intervention can have no one simple answer. The needs and demands of the community, the resources available, and the structure and limitations of the mental health center must all be considered when providing help for each individual client within his community.

REFERENCES

Caplan, Gerald: Principles of preventive psychiatry, New York, 1964, Basic Books, Inc., Publishers.

Christmas, J. J., Wallace, H., and Edwards, J.: New careers and new mental health services; fantasy or future? Am. J. Psychiatry **126:**1480-1486, April 1970.

Clark, Ted, and Jaffe, Dennis T.: Change within youth crisis centers, Am. J. Orthopsychiatry **42:**675-687, July 1972.

Collins, Jerome A.: The paraprofessional. I. Manpower issues in the mental health field, Hosp. Commun. Psychiatry **22:**362-367, Dec. 1971.

Collins, Jerome A., and Cavanaugh, Marilyn:

The paraprofessional. II. Brief mental health training for the community health worker, Hosp. Commun. Psychiatry **22:**367-370, Dec. 1971.

Eastman, K., Coates, D., and Allodi, F.: The concepts of crisis; an expository review, Can. Psychiatr. Assoc. J. **15:**463-472, 1970.

Golan, N.: When is a client in crisis? Social Casework **50:**389-394, July 1969.

Hollingshead, A. B., and Redlich, F. C.: Social class and mental illness, New York, 1958, John Wiley & Sons, Inc.

Janis, Irving L.: Psychological stress, New York, 1958, John Wiley & Sons, Inc.

Rapoport, Lydia: The state of crisis; some

theoretical considerations, Social Service Rev. **36:**211-217, June 1962.

Reiff, Robert: Mental health manpower and community change, Am. Psychologist **21:** 540-548, 1966.

Reissman, C. K.: The supply-demand dilemma in community mental health centers, Am. J. Orthopsychiatry **40:**858-869, Oct. 1970.

Rusk, Thomas: Future changes in mental health care, Hosp. Commun. Psychiatry **22:** 7-9, Jan. 1972.

Schindler-Rainman, Eva: Are volunteers here to stay? Ment. Hyg. **55:**511-515, Oct. 1971.

Sifneos, P. E.: A concept of emotional crisis, Ment. Hyg. **44:**169-179, 1960.

Torop, Paul, and Torop, Karen: Hotlines and youth culture values, Am. J. Psychiatry **129:**106-109, Dec. 1972.

Tyhurst, J. A.: Role of transition states—including disasters—in mental illness, Symposium on Preventive and Social Psychiatry sponsored by Walter Reed Army Institute of Research, Walter Reed Medical Center, and National Research Council, April 15-17, Washington, D. C., 1957, U. S. Government Printing Office.

United States House of Representatives: A bill to provide for the assistance in the construction and initial operation of community mental health centers and for other purposes, #3688, 88th Cong., first sess., 1963.

Van Antwerp, Malin: Primary prevention; a challenge to mental health associations, Ment. Hyg. **54:**453-456, July 1970.

Wilson, S. E., Courtney, C. G., Ota, K. Y., and Radauskas, B.: Evaluating mental health associates, Hosp. Commun. Psychiatry **22:**371-372, Dec. 1971.

ADDITIONAL READINGS

Arnhoff, Franklin N.: Manpower needs, resources and innovation. In Barten, H. H., and Bellak, L., editors: Progress in community mental health, vol. 2, New York, 1972, Grune & Stratton, Inc., pp. 35-61.

Bard, Morton: The role of law enforcement in the helping system, Community Ment. Health J. **7**(2):151-160, 1971.

Barten, H. H., and Bellak, L., editors: Progress in community mental health, vol. 2, New York, 1972, Grune & Stratton, Inc.

Barthal, Hyman S.: Resistances to community psychiatry, Psychiatr. Q. **45**(3):333-343, 1971.

Bindman, Arthur J., and Speigel, Allen D.,

editors: Perspectives in community mental health, Chicago, 1969, Aldine Publishing Co.

Board, Morton: The role of law enforcement in the helping systems, Community Ment. Health J. **7**(2):151-160, 1971.

Brandon, Sydney: Crisis theory and possibilities of therapeutic intervention, Br. J. Psychiatry **117:**541, Dec. 1970.

Bruder, Ernest E.: The clergyman's contribution to community mental health, Hosp. Commun. Psychiatry **22:**207-210, July 1971.

Caplan, Gerald: Practical steps for the family physician, J.A.M.A. **170:**1497-1506, 1959.

Cassell, Wilfred A., and others: Comparing costs of hospital and community care, Hosp. Commun. Psychiatry **23:**197-203, July, 1972.

Chandler, H. M.: Family crisis intervention; point and counterpoint in the psychosocial revolution, J. Natl. Med. Assoc. **64:**211-216, May 1972.

Cobb, C. W.: Community mental health services and the lower socioeconomic classes; a summary of research literature on outpatient treatment (1963-1969), Am. J. Orthopsychiatry **42:**404-414, April 1972.

Daniels, Robert S.: Community psychiatry—a new profession, a developing subspecialty, or effective clinical psychiatry? Community Ment. Health J. **2:**47-54, 1966.

Darbonne, A.: Crisis; a review of theory, practice and research, Int. J. Psychiatry **6:**371-379, Nov. 1968.

Decker, J. B., and Stubblebine, J. M.: Crisis intervention and prevention of disability; a followup study, Am. J. Psychiatry **129:**725-729, Dec. 1972.

de Smit, N. W.: The crisis center in community psychiatry; an Amsterdam experiment. In Masserman, editor: Current psychiatric therapies, vol. 2, New York, 1971, Grune & Stratton, Inc.

de Smit, N. W.: Crisis intervention and crisis centers; their possible relevance for community psychiatry and mental health care, Psychiatr. Neurol. Neurochir. **75:**299-301, 1973.

Edgerton, J. W.: Evaluation in community mental health. In Rosenblum, G., editor: Issues in community psychology and preventive mental health, Task Force on Community Mental Health, Division 27 of the American Psychological Association, New York, 1971, Behavioral Publications, Inc.

Ewalt, J. R., and Farnsworth, D. L.: Psychiatry and religion. In Textbook of psychiatry, New York, 1963, McGraw-Hill Book Co.

Feirstein, A., Weisman, G., and Thomas, C.: A crisis intervention model for inpatient hospitalization. In Masserman, editor: Current psychiatric therapies, vol. 2, New York, 1971, Grune & Stratton, Inc.

Finestone, Samuel, and Sobey, Francine: Nonprofessional personnel in mental health programs, Publication No. 5028, Chevy Chase, Md., 1969, National Clearinghouse for Mental Health Information.

Flomenhaft, K., and others: After the crisis, Ment. Hyg. 55:473-477, Oct. 1971.

Frazier, S. H.: New horizons in psychiatric treatment. I. Goals, processes, and predictions, Hosp. Commun. Psychiatry 19:1-6, Jan. 1968.

Goffman, E.: Asylums, Garden City, N. Y., 1961, Doubleday & Co., Inc.

Gurin, G., Veroff, J., and Feld, S.: Americans view their mental health; a nationwide survey; a report to the staff director, Jack R. Ewalt, New York, 1960, Basic Books, Inc., Publishers.

Hill, Reuben: Social stresses on the family; generic features of families under stress, Social Casework, 39:139-150, 1958.

Huessy, Hans R.: Rural models. In Barten, H. H., and Bellak, L., editors: Progress in community mental health, vol. 2, New York, 1972, Grune & Stratton, Inc., pp. 199-220.

Kelly, James G.: The mental health agent in the community. In Bindman, Arthur J., and Speigel, Allen D., editors: Perspectives in community mental health, Chicago, 1969, Aldine Publishing Co., pp. 620-634.

Lampe, Matthew: Drugs; information for crisis treatment, Belloit, Wis., 1972, Stash Press.

Liberman, Robert: Police as community mental health resources, Community Ment. Health J. 5(2):111-120, 1969.

Mackenzie, M., and others: Family crisis unit, Lancet 1:642, March 1972.

McCann, R. V.: The churches and mental health; a report to the staff director, Jack R. Ewalt, New York, 1962, Basic Books, Inc., Publishers.

McClellan, M. S.: Crisis groups in special care areas, Nurs. Clin. North Am. 7:363-371, June 1972.

Moorehead, M. A.: Evaluating quality of care

of the neighborhood health center program of O.E.O., Med. Care 8:118-131, 1970.

Naylor, Harriet: New trends in volunteer services for the mentally handicapped, Hosp. Commun. Psychiatry 22:109-111, April 1971.

Peterson, Harry: A survey of community helpers, Hosp. Commun. Psychiatry 20:359, Nov. 1969.

Polak, P.: Techniques of social system intervention, Curr. Psychiatr. Ther. 12:185-193, 1972.

Pretzel, P. W.: The volunteer clinical worker at the suicide prevention center, Bull. Suicidology 6:29-34, 1970.

Raphael, Beverly: Crisis intervention; theoretical and methodological considerations, Aust. N. Z. J. Psychiatry 5:183-190, 1971.

Reiff, R., and Reissman, F.: The indigenous nonprofessional, Community Ment. Health J. (monograph no. 1), 1965.

Rubenstein, David: Rehospitalization versus family crisis intervention, Am. J. Psychiatry 129:715-720, Dec. 1972.

Schneider, Benjamine: Preparing general practitioners for community mental health work, Hosp. Commun. Psychiatry 22:346-347, Nov. 1971.

Schwartz, Donald A.: Community mental health in 1972; an assessment. In Barten, H. H., and Bellak, L., editors: Progress in community mental health, vol. 2, New York, 1972, Grune & Stratton, Inc.

Schwartz, J. L.: First national survey of free medical clinics, 1967-1969, HSMHA Health Report 86:775-787, Sept. 1971.

Schwartz, S. L.: A review of crisis intervention programs, Psychiatr. Q. 45:498-508, 1971.

Weinstein, R. M., and Brill, N. Q.: Social class and patients' perceptions of mental illness, Psychiatr. Q. 45(1):35-44, 1971.

Wellisch, D. K., and Gay, G. R.: The walking wounded; emergency psychiatric intervention in a heroin addict population, Drug Forum 1:137-144, Jan. 1972.

Wilson, S. E., Courtney, C. G., Ota, K. Y., and Radauskas, B.: Evaluating mental health associates, Hosp. Commun. Psychiatry 22:371-372, Dec. 1971.

Zelbach, Jean Z.: Crisis in chronic problem families. Psychiatric care of the underprivileged, Int. Psychiatry Clin. 8(2):101-142, 1971.

Index

AGUILERA & MESSICK. Crisis intervention.